T0207563

FIRE ALARM

FIRE ALARM

Reading Walter Benjamin's 'On the Concept of History'

◆

MICHAEL LÖWY

TRANSLATED BY CHRIS TURNER

VERSO

London • New York

This edition published by Verso 2016
First published by Verso 2005
Translation © Chris Turner 2005, 2016
First published as *Walter Benjamin. Avertissement d'incendie*
© Presses Universitaires de France, Paris 2001

1 3 5 7 9 10 8 6 4 2

Verso
UK: 6 Meard Street, London W1F 0EG
US: 388 Atlantic Ave, Brooklyn, NY 11217
versobooks.com

Verso is the imprint of New Left Books

ISBN-13: 978-1-78478-641-0 (PB)
ISBN-13: 978-1-78478-643-4 (US EBK)
ISBN-13: 978-1-78478-642-7 (UK EBK)

British Library Cataloguing in Publication Data
A catalogue record for this book is available from the British Library

Library of Congress Cataloging-in-Publication Data
A catalog record for this book is available from the Library of Congress

Typeset in Bembo by Hewer Text UK Ltd, Edinburgh
Printed in the US

CONTENTS

Walter Benjamin, *c.* 1930.
Photograph: Charlotte Joel. Theodor W. Adorno
Archiv, Frankfurt am Main.

Introduction

Romanticism, Messianism and Marxism in Walter Benjamin's Philosophy of History

Walter Benjamin is an author unlike any other. His fragmentary, unfinished, at times hermetic, often anachronistic and yet, nonetheless, always contemporary work, occupies a singular, even unique, place in the intellectual and political panorama of the twentieth century.

Was he primarily, as Hannah Arendt claimed, a literary critic, an '*homme de lettres*', not a philosopher?[1] I am more inclined to agree with Gershem Scholem that, even when writing about art or literature, he was a philosopher.[2] Adorno's point of view is close to Scholem's, as he explains in an unpublished letter to Hannah Arendt: 'For me what defines Benjamin's significance for my own intellectual existence is axiomatic: the essence of his thought as philosophical thought. I have never been able to see his stuff from another perspective . . . Just how far it distances itself from every traditional conception of philosophy is something I am aware of, of course . . .'[3]

Benjamin's readers, particularly in France, have been concerned mainly with the aesthetic side of his work, and have inclined towards regarding him, first and foremost, as a historian of culture.[4] Now, without neglecting that aspect of his work, we must acknowledge the far wider scope of his thought, which aims to achieve no less than a new understanding of human history. His writings on art and literature can be understood only in relation to this overall vision that illuminates them from within. His thinking forms a whole, in which art, history, culture, politics, literature and theology are inseparable.

We usually classify the various philosophies of history by their progressive or conservative, revolutionary or nostalgic character. Walter Benjamin does not fit into these classifications. He is a revolutionary critic of the philosophy of progress, a Marxist opponent of 'progressivism', a nostalgic who dreams of the future, a Romantic advocate of materialism. He is, in every sense of the word, 'unclassifiable'. Adorno rightly defined him as a thinker 'standing apart from all tendencies'.[5] And his work presents itself, in fact, as a kind of erratic block in the margins of the main schools of contemporary philosophy.

It is futile, then, to attempt to recruit him into one or other of the two main camps contending for hegemony on the stage (or should we say the market?) of ideas: modernism and postmodernism.

Jürgen Habermas seems to hesitate: after condemning Benjamin's anti-evolutionism in his article of 1966 as contrary to historical materialism, he asserts in his *The Philosophical Discourse of Modernity* that Benjamin's polemic against 'the socio-evolutionary levelling off' of historical materialism is directed against the 'degeneration of modernity's consciousness of time' and aims, therefore, at 'renew[ing]' that consciousness. But he does not succeed in integrating into his 'philosophical discourse of modernity' the central Benjaminian concepts, such as the 'now-time' – that authentic instant that interrupts the continuum of history – which seems to him to be manifestly inspired by a 'mixture' of Surrealist experiences and motifs from Jewish mysticism.[6]

It would be an equally impossible task to transform Benjamin into a postmodernist *avant la lettre*. His de-legitimation of the grand narrative of Western modernity, his deconstruction of the discourse of progress and his plea for historical discontinuity are immeasurably far removed from the postmodernists' detached gaze on current society, which is presented as a world where grand narratives have finally been consigned to the past and replaced by 'flexible, agonistic language games'.[7]

Benjamin's conception of history is not postmodern, firstly because, far from being 'beyond all narratives' – supposing that such a thing were possible – it constitutes a heterodox form of the narrative of emancipation: taking its inspiration from Marxist and messianic sources, it uses nostalgia for the past as a revolutionary method for the critique of the present.[8] His thought is, therefore, neither modern (in Habermas's sense) nor 'postmodern' (as Lyotard understands the term), but consists rather in *a modern critique of* (capitalist/ industrial) *modernity*, inspired by pre-capitalist cultural and historical references.

Among the attempts at interpreting his work, there is one that seems to me particularly questionable: the approach that believes he can be placed in the same philosophical camp as Martin Heidegger. In her touching essay of the 1960s, Hannah Arendt unfortunately contributed to this confusion, asserting, against all the evidence, that 'Without realizing it, Benjamin actually had more in common with [Heidegger] . . . than he did with the dialectical subtleties of his Marxist friends.'[9] However, Benjamin made crystal clear his feelings of hostility towards the author of *Sein und Zeit* long before Heidegger revealed his allegiance to the Third Reich. In a letter to Scholem dated 20 January 1930, he speaks of 'the shock of the confrontation between our two very different ways of looking at history' and shortly afterwards, on 25 April, he writes to his friend about a project for a critical reading, with Brecht, in which they 'were planning to annihilate Heidegger'.[10] In *The Arcades Project* he mentions one of the main points of his critique: 'Heidegger seeks in vain to rescue history for phenomenology abstractly through "historicity" (*Geschichtlichkeit*)'.[11] When, in 1938, *Internationale Literatur*, a Moscow-based Stalinist publication, presented him, on the strength of a passage from his article on Goethe's *Wahlverwandschaften* (1922), as a 'follower of Heidegger', he could not help but comment, in a letter to Gretel Adorno (20 July 1938), that 'this publication is quite wretched'.[12]

One may, admittedly, compare the two authors' conceptions of historical time to identify points of affinity: the theme of eschatology, the Heideggerian conception of 'authentic temporality', and the openness of the past. If one takes the view, as Lucien Goldmann does, that Lukács's *History and Class Consciousness* was one of the hidden sources of *Being and Time*,[13] one might suppose that Benjamin and Heidegger both drew inspiration from the same work. However, starting out from a set of common questions, the two thinkers diverge radically. It seems clear to me that Benjamin was not a 'follower' of Heidegger, not simply because he denies it categorically, but for the good reason that his critical conception of temporality was already defined, to all intents and purposes, during the years 1915–25, long before the publication of *Sein und Zeit* in 1927.

Walter Benjamin's 'Theses "On the Concept of History"' (1940) constitutes one of the most important philosophical and political texts of the twentieth century. In revolutionary thought, it is perhaps the most significant document since Marx's 'Theses on Feuerbach'. It is an enigmatic, allusive, even sybilline text, its hermeticism studded with images, allegories and illuminations, strewn with strange paradoxes and shot through with dazzling insights.

If we are to be able to interpret this document, it is, I believe, indispensable to situate it within the development of Benjamin's work. Let us attempt to identify, in the movement of his thought, the moments that prepare or prefigure the text of 1940.

Benjamin's philosophy of history draws on three very different sources: German Romanticism, Jewish messianism and Marxism. And we are not looking at a combinatorial or an eclectic 'synthesis' of these three (apparently) incompatible perspectives, but at the invention of a new and profoundly original conception on the basis of all of them. His approach cannot be explained by some particular 'influence': the different schools of thought, the various authors he cites and his friends' writings are so many materials from which he builds a construction of his own, elements with which he effects an alchemical fusion to produce philosophers' gold.

The expression 'philosophy of history' may be misleading here. There is no philosophical system in Benjamin's writings: all his thinking takes the form of essays or fragments, if not indeed of quotation pure and simple – the passages wrenched from their context being made to serve his own approach. Any attempt at systematizing this mode of 'thinking poetically' (Hannah Arendt) is, then, problematical and uncertain. The brief remarks that follow merely offer a number of avenues for research.

In the literature on Benjamin one often finds two symmetrical errors that should, I think, be avoided at all costs. The first consists in splitting off the 'idealist', 'theological' work of his youth from the 'materialist' revolutionary work of his maturity by effecting a (quasi-surgical) 'epistemological break' between the two. The second, by contrast, sees his work as a homogeneous whole and takes no account whatever of the profound upheaval occasioned in the mid-1920s by his discovery of Marxism. In order to understand the movement of his thought, we have, then, to take account simultaneously of the continuity of certain essential themes and the various breaks and turning points that mark his intellectual and political trajectory.[14]

Let us take as our starting point the Romantic moment, which is at the centre of the preoccupations of the young Benjamin. To grasp the full scope of this, we have perhaps to remember that Romanticism is not just a literary and artistic school of the early nineteenth century: it is a true vision of the world, a style of thinking, a structure of sensibility that manifests itself in all spheres of cultural life, from Rousseau and Novalis to the Surrealists (and beyond). One might define the Romantic *Weltanschauung* as a cultural critique of modern (capitalist) civilization in the name of pre-modern (pre-capitalist) values – a critique or protest that bears upon aspects which are felt to be unbearable and degrading: the quantification and mechanization of life, the reification of social relations, the dissolution of the community and the disenchantment of the world. Its nostalgia for the past does not mean it is necessarily retrograde: the Romantic view of the world may assume both reactionary and revolutionary forms. For revolutionary Romanticism the aim is not a *return* to the past, but a *detour* through the past on the way to a utopian future.[15]

In late nineteenth-century Germany, Romanticism (sometimes referred to as 'neo-Romanticism') was one of the dominant cultural forms in both literature and the human sciences; it expresses itself through multiple attempts at *re-enchanting the world*, in which the 'return of the religious element' plays a pre-eminent role. Benjamin's relation to Romanticism is not, then, expressed solely either through his interest in the *Frühromantik* (in particular Schlegel and Novalis) or in such late Romantic figures as E. T. A. Hoffmann, Franz von Baader, Franz-Joseph Molitor and Johann Jakob Bachofen – or, alternatively, in Baudelaire and the Surrealists – but through the whole range of his aesthetic, theological and historiosophical ideas. Moreover, these three spheres are so closely connected in Benjamin that it is difficult to dissociate them without destroying what constitutes the singularity of his thinking.

And, indeed, one of Benjamin's first articles (published in 1913) was entitled *Romantik*: it calls for the birth of a new Romanticism, proclaiming

that the 'Romantic will to beauty, the Romantic will to truth', and 'the
Romantic will to action' are the 'unsurpassable' achievements of modern
culture. This virtually inaugural text attests both to Benjamin's deep attach-
ment to the Romantic tradition – conceived as art, knowledge and praxis –
and to a desire for renewal.[16]

Another narrative from the same period – the 'Dialogue on the Religiosity
of the Present' – also reveals the young Benjamin's fascination for this culture:
'We have had Romanticism and we owe to it the powerful insight into the
nocturnal side of the natural . . . But we live as though Romanticism had
never existed.' The text also touches on the neo-Romantic longing for a new
religion and a new socialism, whose prophets are Tolstoy, Nietzsche and
Strindberg. This 'social religion' is said to be opposed to the current
conceptions of the social sphere, which reduce it to 'a matter of *Zivilisation*,
like electric light'. The dialogue here takes up several aspects of the Romantic
critique of modernity: the transformation of human beings into 'work
machines', the degradation of work into mere technique, the hope-sapping
subjection of persons to the social mechanism, the replacement of the 'heroic
– revolutionary – efforts' of the past by the pitiful (crab-like) march of
evolution and progress.[17]

This last remark already shows us the twist Benjamin imparts to the
Romantic tradition: the attack on the ideology of progress is not made in the
name of backward-looking conservatism, but of revolution. We find this
subversive inflection again in his lecture on 'The Life of Students' (1914), a
key document which seems to gather into a single beam of light all the ideas
that will stay with him throughout his life. According to Benjamin, the real
questions facing society are not 'limited technical philosophical matters
but . . . the great metaphysical questions of Plato and Spinoza, the Romantics
and Nietzsche'.[18] Among these 'metaphysical' questions, that of historical
temporality is essential. The remarks that open the essay provide a striking
foretaste of his messianic philosophy of history:

> There is a view of history that puts its faith in the infinite extent of time and
> thus concerns itself only with the speed, or lack of it, with which people
> and epochs advance along the path of progress. This corresponds to a
> certain absence of coherence and rigor in the demands it makes on the

present. The following remarks, in contrast, delineate a particular condition in which history appears to be concentrated in a single focal point, like those that have traditionally been found in the utopian images of the philosophers.

The elements of the ultimate condition do not manifest themselves as formless progressive tendencies, but are deeply rooted in every present in the form of the most endangered, excoriated, and ridiculed ideas and products of the creative mind . . . This condition cannot be captured in terms of the pragmatic description of details . . . Rather, the task is to grasp its metaphysical structure, as with the messianic domain or the idea of the French Revolution.[19]

Utopian (messianic or revolutionary) images against 'formless progressive tendencies' – posed here in a nutshell are the terms of the debate Benjamin will continue to conduct throughout his life. *Messianism* is, in Benjamin's view, at the heart of the Romantic conception of time and history. In the introduction to his doctoral thesis, 'The Concept of Criticism in German Romanticism' (1919), he stresses the idea that the historic essence of Romanticism is to be 'sought in Romantic messianism'. He discovers this dimension particularly in the writings of Schlegel and Novalis and quotes, among others, this remarkable passage from the young Friedrich Schlegel: 'The revolutionary desire to realize the kingdom of God on earth is . . . the inception of modern history.'[20] We come back here to the 'metaphysical' question of historical temporality: Benjamin ranges the qualitative conception of infinite time (*qualitative zeitliche Unendlichkeit*) 'which derives from Romantic messianism', and for which the life of humanity is a process of *accomplishment* and not merely of becoming, against the infinitely *empty* time (*leeren Unendlichkeit der Zeit*) characteristic of the modern ideology of progress. One cannot but note the striking similarity between this passage, which seems to have escaped the attention of the commentators, and the 1940 'Theses "On the Concept of History"'.[21]

What is the relationship between the two 'utopian images', the messianic kingdom and revolution? Without directly answering this question, Benjamin addresses it in a text, unpublished in his lifetime, which probably dates from 1921 to 1922: the so-called 'Theological-Political Fragment'. Initially, he seems radically to distinguish the sphere of historical becoming from that of the Messiah: 'Nothing that is historical can relate itself, from its own ground, to anything messianic.'[22] Immediately thereafter, however, he throws a dialectical bridge across this apparently unbridgeable abyss, a fragile gangway that seems directly inspired by certain paragraphs in Franz Rosenzweig's *The Star of Redemption* (1921), a book Benjamin held in the highest esteem. The dynamics of the secular order, which he defines as 'the quest of free humanity for happiness' – to be compared with Rosenzweig's 'great works of liberation' – may promote 'the coming of the Messianic Kingdom'. If Benjamin's formulation is less explicit than Rosenzweig's, for whom emancipatory acts are 'the necessary condition for the advent of the Kingdom of God', the procedure is the same, seeking to establish a mediation between the liberatory, historic, 'secular' struggles of human beings and the fulfilment of the messianic promise.[23]

How will this messianic, utopian and Romantic ferment articulate itself with historical materialism? It was from 1924 onwards, when he read Lukács's *History and Class Consciousness* and discovered Communism through the eyes of Asja Lacis, that Marxism began to become a key element in his conception of history. In 1929, Benjamin was still referring to Lukács's essay as one of the few books that remained lively and contemporary:

> The most finished [*geschlossenste*] philosophical work of Marxist literature. Its singularity lies in the assurance with which it has grasped, on the one hand, the critical situation of the class struggle in the critical situation of philosophy and, on the other, revolution, now concretely due, as the absolute precondition, if not indeed the absolute fulfilment and completion, of theoretical knowledge.[24]

This text shows the aspect of Marxism that most interests Benjamin and which will enable us to cast new light on his vision of the historical process: *class struggle*. But historical materialism will not supplant his Romantically and messianically inspired 'anti-progressive' intuitions: it will articulate itself with them, thus acquiring a critical quality that marks it off radically from the then dominant 'official' Marxism. By his critical attitude to the ideology of progress, Benjamin in fact occupies a peculiar, unique position in Marxist thinking and in the European Left in the inter-war years.[25]

This articulation first emerges in *One-Way Street*, written between 1923 and 1926, where we find, under the heading 'Fire Alarm', this historical premonition of the threats posed by progress: if the overthrow of the bourgeoisie by the proletariat 'is not completed by an almost calculable moment in economic and technical development (a moment signalled by inflation and poison-gas warfare), all is lost. Before the spark reaches the dynamite, the lighted fuse must be cut.'[26]

Contrary to vulgar evolutionary Marxism – which is, admittedly, able to point to sources in some of the writings of Marx and Engels themselves – Benjamin does not conceive revolution as the 'natural' or 'inevitable' outcome of economic and technical progress (or of the 'contradiction between the forces and relations of production'), but as the interruption of a process of historical evolution leading to catastrophe. It is because he perceives this catastrophic danger that he speaks up (in his 1929 article on Surrealism) for pessimism – for a revolutionary pessimism that has nothing to do with fatalistic resignation and even less with the conservative, reactionary, pre-fascist German *Kulturpessimismus* of Carl Schmitt, Oswald Spengler or Moeller van den Bruck. Benjamin's pessimism is in the service of the oppressed classes. His preoccupation is not with the 'decline' of the elites or the nation, but with the threats the technical and economic progress fostered by capitalism pose for humanity.

Nothing seems more derisory to Benjamin than the *optimism* of the bourgeois parties and Social Democracy, whose political programme is merely 'a bad poem on springtime'. Against this 'unprincipled dilettantish optimism', inspired by the ideology of linear progress, he discovers in pessimism the point of effective convergence between Surrealism and Communism.[27] Needless to say, this is not a contemplative sentiment, but an active, 'organized', practical pessimism, directed entirely at preventing the onset of disaster by all possible means.

One wonders what the concept of pessimism applied to the Communists might possibly be referring to: is not their doctrine in 1929, celebrating the triumphs of the building of socialism in the USSR and the imminent fall of capitalism, precisely a fine example of the optimistic illusion? In fact, Benjamin borrowed the concept of the 'organization of pessimism' from a work he describes as 'excellent' – *La Révolution et les intellectuels* (1928) by the dissident Communist Pierre Naville. Naville, a member of the Surrealist group – he had been one of the editors of the journal *La Révolution surréaliste* – had at that point decided to commit himself to the French Communist Party and sought to persuade his friends to do the same. Now, for Naville, the pessimism that constitutes 'the source of Marx's revolutionary method' is the only way of 'escaping the mediocrity and disappointment of an age of compromise'. Rejecting the 'crude optimism' of a Herbert Spencer – whom he fondly describes as a 'monstrously shrivelled brain' – or an Anatole France, whose loathsome jokes he detests, he concludes: 'we must organize pessimism'; 'the organization of pessimism' is the only slogan that will prevent us from withering away.[28]

We scarcely need add that this passionate defence of pessimism was far from representative of the political culture of French Communism in this period. In fact, Pierre Naville was soon to be expelled from the party (1928): the logic of his anti-optimism would lead him into the ranks of the Trotskyist Left opposition, one of whose main leaders he was to become.

In Benjamin's work, the pessimistic philosophy of history shows up with particular acuteness in his vision of the future of Europe:

> . . . pessimism all along the line. Absolutely. Mistrust in the fate of literature, mistrust in the fate of freedom, mistrust in the fate of European humanity, but three times mistrust in all reconciliation: between classes, between nations, between individuals. And unlimited trust only in IG Farben and the peaceful perfecting of the air force.[29]

This critical vision enabled Benjamin to foresee – intuitively, but with a strange acuity – the catastrophes awaiting Europe, perfectly summed up in the ironic phrase on 'unlimited trust'. Naturally, even he, the most pessimistic of all, could not predict the destruction the German air force was to wreak on the cities and civilian populations of Europe; that IG Farben would, barely a dozen years later, distinguish itself by the manufacture of the Zyklon B gas used to 'rationalize' genocide; or that its factories would employ labour from the concentration camps by the tens of thousands. However, uniquely among the Marxist thinkers and leaders of these years, Benjamin had a premonition of the monstrous disasters to which a crisis-ridden industrial-bourgeois civilization could give birth.[30]

This pessimism manifests itself in Benjamin, as it did in Blanqui or Péguy, in a kind of 'revolutionary melancholia', which betrays a sense of a recurrence of disaster, the fear of an eternal return of defeats.[31] How is it reconciled with his commitment to the cause of the oppressed? Benjamin's 'proletarian' choice was in no way inspired by any kind of optimism regarding the behaviour of the 'masses' or a confidence in the brilliant future of socialism. It is essentially a *wager*, in the Pascalian sense, on the possibility of a struggle for emancipation.

The 1929 article attests to Benjamin's interest in Surrealism, which he sees as a modern manifestation of revolutionary Romanticism. We might perhaps define the approach common to Benjamin and André Breton as a kind of 'Gothic Marxism', distinct from the dominant version that was metaphysically materialistic in tendency and contaminated by the evolutionary ideology of progress.[32] The adjective 'Gothic' has to be understood in its Romantic sense: fascination with enchantment and the marvellous, and also with the enchanted [*ensorcelés*] aspects of pre-modern societies and cultures. The English Gothic novel of the eighteenth century and some of the German Romantics of the nineteenth are 'Gothic' references one finds at the heart of the work of Breton and Benjamin.

The Gothic Marxism common to the two men might be said, then, to be a historical materialism sensitive to the magical dimension of the cultures of the past, to the 'dark' moment of revolt, to the lightning flash that rends the heavens of revolutionary action. 'Gothic' is also to be taken in the literal sense of a positive reference to certain key moments in secular medieval culture: it is no accident that both Breton and Benjamin admire the courtly love of the Middle Ages in Provence, which, in the eyes of the latter, represents one of the purest manifestations of profane illumination.[33]

For a brief 'experimental' period between 1933 and 1935, during the years of the Second Five-Year Plan, some of Benjamin's Marxist texts seem close to 'Soviet productivism' and an uncritical adherence to the promises of technological progress.[34] However, even in these years he had not quite lost his interest in the Romantic problematic, as his 1935 article on Bachofen attests. In fact, Benjamin's thinking in this period is quite contradictory: he sometimes shifts very quickly from one extreme to the other – even in a single text, as in the famous essay on the work of art. One finds in these writings both a permanent aspect of his Marxist thinking – the materialist preoccupation –

and an 'experimental' tendency to push certain arguments to their ultimate consequences. He seems tempted by a Soviet variant of the ideology of progress, though reinterpreted in his own way. Some Marxist readings of Benjamin's works foreground just these texts that are closer to a 'classical', if not orthodox, historical materialism. If I take the opposite stance, this is both because of my own interests and philosophical and political options, and on account of the genesis of the 1940 'Theses', which take their main inspiration from other writings.

After 1936, this kind of 'progressive parenthesis' closes again and Benjamin increasingly reintegrates the Romantic moment into his *sui generis* Marxist critique of the capitalist forms of alienation. For example, in his 1936–38 writings on Baudelaire, he takes up again the typically Romantic idea – suggested in a 1930 essay on E. T. A. Hoffmann[35] – of the radical opposition between life and the automaton in the context of a Marxist-inspired analysis of the transformation of the proletarian into an automaton. The repetitive, meaningless, mechanical gestures of the worker grappling with the machine – Benjamin refers here to certain passages from Marx's *Capital* – are similar to the automaton-like gestures of passers-by in the crowd, as described by Poe and Hoffmann. Both groups of people, as victims of urban, industrial civilization, no longer know authentic experience (*Erfahrung*) – based on the memory of a historical, cultural tradition – but only immediate life (*Erlebnis*), and in particular the '*Chockerlebnis*' that produces in them a reactive behaviour, akin to that of automata 'who have completely liquidated their memory'.[36]

The Romantic protest against capitalist modernity is always made in the name of an idealized past, real or mythical. What is the past that serves as a reference for the Marxist Walter Benjamin in his critique of bourgeois civilization and the illusions of progress? In the theological writings of his youth, there are frequent references to a lost paradise, but in the 1930s primitive communism comes to play this role – as, indeed, it does for Marx and Engels, who were attentive readers of the Romantic anthropology of Maurer and Bachofen, as well as the works of Morgan.

The review of Bachofen's work that Benjamin wrote in 1935 is one of the most important keys for understanding his method of constructing a new philosophy of history on the basis of Marxism and Romanticism.[37] He writes that Bachofen's work, drawing on 'Romantic sources', fascinated Marxists and anarchists (like Élisée Reclus) by its 'evocation of a communistic society at the dawn of history'.[38] Rejecting conservative (Klages) and fascist (Bäumler) interpretations, Benjamin stresses that Bachofen 'had explored to previously unplumbed depths the sources which, through the ages, had fed the libertarian ideal which Reclus espoused'.[39] As for Engels and Paul Lafargue, their interest was also attracted by Bachofen's work on matriarchal societies, in which there was apparently a high degree of democracy and civic equality, together with forms of primitive communism that thoroughly 'overturned the concept of authority'.[40]

Similar ideas were outlined in his essays on Baudelaire: Benjamin interpreted the '*vie antérieure*' evoked by the poet as a reference to a primitive, edenic age in which authentic experience still existed and in which ritual and festivities allowed for a fusion between the past of the individual and the collective past. Such, then, is the *Erfahrung* that feeds the play of 'correspondences' in Baudelaire's work and inspires his rejection of the modern catastrophe: 'The important thing is that the *correspondances* record a concept of experience which includes ritual elements. Only by appropriating these elements was Baudelaire able to fathom the full meaning of the breakdown which he, a modern man, was witnessing.' These 'ritual elements' relate to a distant past, similar to the societies studied by Bachofen: '*Correspondances* are the data of remembrance – not historical data, but data of prehistory. What makes festive days great and significant is the encounter with an earlier life.'[41] Rolf Tiedemann very aptly observes that, for Benjamin, 'the idea of correspondences is the utopia by which a lost paradise appears projected into the future'.[42]

It was above all in the various texts of the years 1936–40 that Benjamin would develop his vision of history, dissociating himself more and more radically from the 'illusions of progress' that retained their hegemonic grip on the German and European Left. In a long essay published in 1937 in the *Zeitschrift für Sozialforschung*, the journal of the Frankfurt School (already exiled to the United States), on the work of the historian and collector Eduard Fuchs – which contains entire passages that foreshadow, sometimes word for word, the 1940 'Theses' – he attacks Social Democratic Marxism, a mix of positivism, Darwinian evolutionism and the cult of progress: 'In the

development of technology, it [positivism] was able to see only the progress
of natural science, not the concomitant regression of society . . . The energies
that technology develops beyond this threshold are destructive. First of all,
they advance the technology of war and its propagandistic preparation.'[43]
Among the most striking examples of this blinkered positivism, he cites the
Italian socialist Enrico Ferri, who sought to trace not just 'the principles', but
'even the tactics of Social Democracy back to natural laws', and who imputed
anarchistic tendencies within the labour movement to 'deficiencies in the
knowledge of geology and biology'.[44]

Benjamin's objective was to deepen and radicalise the opposition between
Marxism and the bourgeois philosophies of history, to sharpen its revolutionary thrust and raise its critical content. It is in this spirit that he trenchantly
defines the aim of *The Arcades Project*: 'It may be considered one of the
methodological objectives of this work to demonstrate a historical materialism which has annihilated within itself the idea of progress. Just here,
historical materialism has every reason to distinguish itself sharply from
bourgeois habits of thought.'[45] Such a programme did not imply any kind
of 'revisionism', but rather, as Karl Korsch had attempted in his own book –
one of Benjamin's principal references – a return to Marx himself.

Benjamin was aware that this reading of Marxism had its roots in the
Romantic critique of industrial civilization, but he was convinced that Marx
too had taken his inspiration from that source. He found support for this
heretical interpretation of the origins of Marxism in Korsch's *Karl Marx*
(1938):

> Very correctly, and the point is reminiscent of de Maistre and Bonald,
> Korsch says, 'So into the . . . theory of the modern labour movement
> too . . . there went an element of that . . . "disillusionment" which . . .
> after the Great French Revolution, was proclaimed by the first theorists of
> counter-revolution and then by the German Romantics and which, thanks
> to Hegel, strongly influenced Marx'.[46]

It is clear that Benjamin's Marxism, particularly after the years 1936–37,
had little in common with the Soviet 'Diamat' that Stalin was soon (1938) to
codify in a chapter of the very official *History of the Communist Party of the
Soviet Union (Bolsheviks)*. The choice of Karl Korsch as a philosophical

reference – a heterodox Marxist, close to 'Council Communism', expelled from the German Communist Party in the 1920s and radically opposed to the theoretical canons of both Social Democracy and Stalinist Communism – is in itself indicative of this dissidence.

Another example of his autonomy from Stalinism – not necessarily linked with the question of Romanticism – is his interest in Trotsky. In a letter to Gretel Adorno in 1932, he wrote of the autobiography of the founder of the Red Army that it had been years since he had 'consumed anything with such breathtaking excitement'. And Jean Selz, who knew him in Ibiza in 1932, reports that he was in favour of 'a distinctly anti-Stalinistic' Marxism and 'was a great admirer of Trotsky'.[47] If during the years 1933–35 he seems won over, somewhat uncritically, to the Soviet model – perhaps as a reaction to the triumph of Hitlerian Fascism in Germany – and if at the beginning of the Moscow trials he chiefly showed perplexity – 'I cannot make head or tail of it', he wrote to Horkheimer on 31 August 1936[48] – from 1937 to 1938 onwards he distances himself clearly from the Stalinist variant of Communism.

A note on Brecht from this period attests to this development, partly under the influence of Heinrich Blücher (Hannah Arendt's husband), a supporter of the German Communist opposition led by Heinrich Brandler.[49] In that note, he writes of 'GPU practices' and 'procedures in which the worst elements of the Communist Party resonate with the most unscrupulous ones of National Socialism'. Benjamin criticizes Brecht for having, in some poems in the *Lesebuch für Städtebewohner*, 'poetically transfigur[ed] the dangerous and momentous errors into which GPU practices have led the workers' movement', and he criticizes his own commentary on this text by Brecht as a 'pious falsification'.[50]

In spite of this merciless settling of accounts, which does not hesitate to compare Stalinist police practices with those of the Nazis, he still retains one last hope: that the USSR will remain the ally of the anti-Fascists. In a letter to Max Horkheimer, dated 3 August 1938, he demonstrates the hope, 'with a great many reservations', that the Soviet regime – which he openly describes as a 'personal dictatorship with all its terror' – can still be considered, 'at least for the moment', as 'the agent of our interests in a future war'. He adds that it is a question of an agent that 'costs the highest price imaginable insofar as it has to be paid for with sacrifices that most particularly erode the interests that are dear to us as producers' – an expression which doubtless refers to the emancipation of the workers and socialism.[51]

The Molotov–Ribbentrop Pact was to deal this last illusion a heavy blow. The 'Theses "On the Concept of History"' were composed in this new context.

The chapter 'Fire Alarm' in *One-Way Street* is one of Benjamin's most impressive texts. But, in a sense, his whole work can be regarded as a kind of 'fire alarm' to his contemporaries, a warning bell attempting to draw attention to the imminent dangers threatening them, to the new catastrophes looming on the horizon. The 1940 'Theses' are the dense, compact expression of this approach and this disquiet.

I

A Reading of Walter Benjamin's
'Theses "On the Concept of History"'

Before moving on to a 'talmudic' analysis of Benjamin's text – word by word and sentence by sentence – a few short remarks are in order as an introduction to the reading of the 'Theses'. The document 'On the Concept of History' was written in the early days of 1940, shortly before its author's attempt to escape from Vichy France, where Jewish and/or Marxist German refugees were handed over by the authorities to the Gestapo. As we know, that attempt failed: intercepted by Franco's police at the Spanish border (Port-Bou) in September 1940, Walter Benjamin chose suicide.

The first reference to the document appears in a letter from Benjamin to Adorno, written in French, on 22 February 1940. This explains the aim of the text to his friend: to 'establish an irremediable break [*scission*] between our way of seeing and the survivals of positivism', which haunt even the historical conceptions of the Left.[1] To Benjamin, positivism appears, then, as the common denominator of the tendencies he will criticize: conservative historicism, Social Democratic evolutionism and vulgar Marxism.[2]

We must make clear that the document was not intended for publication. Benjamin gave it or sent it to a number of very close friends, such as Hannah Arendt and Theodor Adorno, but he stressed, in the letter to Gretel Adorno, that there was no question of publishing it, as 'that would throw wide open the doors to enthusiastic incomprehension'.[3] His prophetic fears were fully realized: much of the literature on the 'Theses' displays incomprehension,

Cemetery, Port-Bou.

some of it enthusiastic, some of it sceptical, but, in any event, incapable of grasping the significance of the text.

The direct spur to composing the 'Theses' was doubtless the Germano-Soviet Pact, the outbreak of the Second World War and the occupation of Europe by Nazi troops. But it was, nonetheless, the summation – the ultimate, concentrated expression – of ideas that run through the whole of his work. In one of his last letters, addressed to Gretel Adorno, Benjamin writes: 'War and the combination of circumstances that brought it about have led me to put down on paper some thoughts about which I may say that I have kept them about myself – and even from myself – for some twenty years.' He could have written 'twenty-five years' since, as we have seen, the lecture on 'The Life of Students' (1914) already contained some of the key ideas of his spiritual testament of 1940.[4]

We have, then, to situate the document in its historical context. It was, to use Victor Serge's expression, 'midnight in the century' and that terrible

moment of contemporary history doubtless represents the immediate back-
ground to the text. However, we cannot for all that see it solely as the product
of a precise conjuncture: it bears a significance that far exceeds the tragic
constellation that gave birth to it. If it still speaks to us today, if it arouses so
much interest, so many discussions and polemics, this is because, through the
prism of a determinate historic moment, it raises questions that bear on the
whole of modern history and on the place of the twentieth century in the
social development of humanity.

The history of the 'rescue' and publication of the 'Theses' has been
minutely reconstructed by the editors of the *Gesammelte Schriften*. It was a
copy given by Benjamin to Hannah Arendt and passed on by her to Adorno
that was first printed in a kind of mimeographed booklet entitled *Walter
Benjamin zum Gedächtnis* (In memory of Walter Benjamin) which was
intended for a relatively limited audience. A few hundred copies of this
were printed in 1942 by the Frankfurt Institute of Social Research, exiled in
the USA.

Paradoxically, the first publication, in the full sense of the term, was in
French, in Pierre Missac's translation, and this appeared in October 1947 in
Les Temps modernes (25, pp. 623–34). It provoked no reaction. The same
absence of response followed the publication in German, through Adorno's
good offices, in the journal *Neue Rundschau* (4, pp. 560–70) in 1950. It was
only after the appearance of the text in the first collection of Benjamin's
writings edited by Adorno – *Schriften* (Frankfurt: Suhrkamp, 1955) – that the
reception of the document and the first discussions really began. Finally, in
1974, the critical edition of the 'Theses', variants and notes, with a commentary – together with the French translation made by Benjamin himself –
appeared in the *Gesammelte Schriften* (Frankfurt: Suhrkamp), edited by R.
Tiedemann and H. Schweppenhäuser, with the collaboration of Adorno and
Scholem. To this we have to add the last copy, entitled *Handexemplar* (which
has the peculiarity of converting one of the preparatory notes into Thesis
XVIII), discovered by Giorgio Agamben and incorporated into volume VII
of the *Gesammelte Schriften* (1991).

In the debates which, from the 1950s onwards, followed the publication of
the 'Theses', we may distinguish three main schools of interpretation:

1. *The materialist school*: Walter Benjamin is a Marxist, a coherent materialist. His theological formulations have to be regarded as metaphors, as an exotic form in which materialist truths are clothed. This was the position adopted by Brecht as early as his 'Working Journal'.[5]

2. *The theological school*: Walter Benjamin is, first and foremost, a Jewish theologian, a messianic thinker. His Marxism is merely a terminology and he falsely appropriates such concepts as 'historical materialism'. This was the view of his friend Gershom Scholem.

3. *The school of contradiction*: Walter Benjamin tries to reconcile Marxism with Jewish theology, materialism with messianism. Now, as everyone knows, the two are incompatible. Hence the failure of his endeavour. This is the reading shared by Jürgen Habermas and Rolf Tiedemann.

In my view, these three schools of thought are simultaneously right and wrong. I should like, modestly, to propose a fourth approach. Walter Benjamin is a Marxist *and* a theologian. It is true that these two conceptions are usually contradictory. But the author of the 'Theses' is not a 'usual' thinker: he reinterprets these conceptions, transforms them and situates them in a relation of reciprocal illumination that enables them to be articulated together in a coherent way. He liked to compare himself to a Janus figure, one of whose faces was turned towards Moscow and the other towards Jerusalem. But what is often forgotten is that the Roman god had two faces but a single head: Marxism and messianism are simply two expressions – *Ausdrücke*, one of Benjamin's favourite terms – of a single thought. An innovative, original, unclassifiable thought, characterized by what he calls, in a letter to Scholem of May 1926, the 'sudden paradoxical change of one form of [religious or political] observance into the other (regardless of which direction)'.[6] The better to grasp the complex and subtle relationship between redemption and revolution in his philosophy of history, we should speak of an *elective affinity* or, in other words, of a mutual attraction and reciprocal reinforcement of the two approaches, on the basis of certain structural analogies, leading to a kind of alchemical fusion – like the amorous encounter between two souls in Goethe's novel, *Die Wahlverwandschaften*, to which Benjamin had devoted one of the most important of the essays of his youth.[7]

Though Scholem's unilateral approach must necessarily be criticized, we should not underestimate the deep attraction his thinking exerted on Benjamin, including at the time when he was writing the 'Theses'. An as yet unpublished document that I have been able to consult in the Scholem Archive at the library of the Hebrew University shows without a shadow of a doubt that the very title of the 'Theses' was inspired by an unpublished manuscript of Scholem's, which Benjamin doubtless knew, entitled *Thesen über den Begriff der Gerechtigkeit* (Theses on the Concept of Justice), dated 1919 and 1925. Reading this text, one realizes that Benjamin was not just inspired by the title, but also by the content of the manuscript. Take, for example, the following passage: 'The messianic age as eternal present and the justice of the − substantial − existent [*Daseiendes*] correspond to one another [*entsprechen sich*]. If justice were not *there*, the Messianic Kingdom not only would not be there, but would be impossible.'[8]

The objective of the notes and comments that follow is not so much to 'judge' Benjamin's theses as to attempt to understand them. This will not prevent me from paying homage to his lucidity or, where necessary, criticizing what seems questionable. The interpretation proposed does not seek to be exhaustive; even less does it claim to be the most 'correct', the 'truest' or the most 'scientific'. At best it attempts to bring out a certain coherence where so many others merely see dissonance, contradiction or ambiguity.

Benjamin's concepts are not metaphysical abstractions, but relate to concrete historical experiences. I have, therefore, chosen to illustrate his remarks with examples − both from modern European and ancient Jewish history − inspired, directly or indirectly, by his own writings. I have also added a number of contemporary Latin American examples. Though this may initially be surprising, it seems to me that this addresses an important issue pointing up both the universality and the topicality of Walter Benjamin's concept of history. I came upon the 'Theses' at the point when popular insurrectional movements were developing in central America: the document enabled me to understand these events better and, conversely, they shed a new light on the text.

For the original French edition of this work I took as my starting point Maurice de Gandillac's sober and elegant translation published in 1971 by

Éditions Maurice Nadeau in the collection of Benjamin's essays entitled *Poésie et vérité*, even though it is imprecise at a considerable number of points.[9] I also often drew on the incomplete, but infinitely precious translation drafted by Benjamin himself, which differs in certain respects from the German text and hence constitutes something of a variant. Lastly, following the example of Italian scholars, I have added to the known list of theses a new one that figures as number XVIII in the copy discovered some years ago by Giorgio Agamben.[10] This thesis already appeared among the preparatory notes published in the *Gesammelte Schriften* as number XVIIa. The *Handexemplar* found by Agamben shows that Benjamin intended to include it in the final version of the document. It is, indeed, an autonomous text of the greatest importance, and not a variant. It figures here as Thesis XVIIa, to avoid changing the accepted numbering of the last theses.

For the interpretation of the 'Theses', I have often referred to the preparatory notes, published in volume I, 3 of the *Gesammelte Schriften*, some of which are available in English translation as 'Paralipomena to "On the Concept of History"'.[11]

A few personal remarks to close this introduction. I discovered the 'Theses "On the Concept of History"' belatedly. Paradoxically, it was thanks to the writings of Gershom Scholem, whom I met in Jerusalem in 1979, that I became aware of this document, at a point when I was becoming interested in the relations between messianism and utopianism in Judaism. Yet the text had been available in French since 1947 and in German since 1950. I do not know whether this delay is to be attributed to ignorance, blindness or misjudgement. In any event, there is, in my intellectual itinerary, a before and an after the discovery of the *Thesen "Über den Begriff der Geschichte"*.

Since I read the text some twenty years ago, it has continued to haunt, fascinate, intrigue and move me. I have read it, reread it and reread it again tens of times, with the sense – or the illusion – at each rereading of discovering new aspects, of delving deeper into the infinite density of the text, of at last understanding what, just a short time ago, still seemed hermetic and opaque. I admit that there are still zones of shade for me in some passages, while others seem blinding in their clarity, their inner luminosity, their incontestable self-evidence. These differences show themselves in the very unequal treatment of the theses in my commentary.

Above all, however, the reading of 'Theses' has shaken my certainties, upset my hypotheses, overturned (some of) my firmly held beliefs: in short, it has forced me to think *differently* on a whole string of fundamental questions: progress, religion, history, utopianism and politics. Nothing has emerged unscathed from this crucial encounter.

Gradually, I have also come to realize the universal scope of Benjamin's propositions, their relevance in understanding – 'from the standpoint of the defeated' – not just the history of the oppressed classes, but also that of women (half of humanity), of Jews, Gypsies, American Indians, Kurds, blacks, sexual minorities – in a word, of the pariahs (in the sense Hannah Arendt gave to this term) of all ages and all continents.

Over the last fifteen years I have made a great many notes for an interpretation of the 'Theses'. I have followed the courses and lectures of such eminent specialists as Stéphane Mosès and Irving Wohlfarth. I also devoted a year's seminar at the EHESS to the 'Theses' and, later, another at the University of São Paolo in Brazil. I have read a large proportion of the 'secondary literature', but I remain convinced not only that there is still room for other interpretations – such as the one I propose here – but that Benjamin's text belongs to that rare species of writings whose destiny it is to prompt new readings, new viewpoints, different hermeneutic approaches and original thoughts *ad infinitum*. Or rather, as the Shema Israel, the age-old prayer of the Jews, puts it, *le'olem va'ed* – for ever.

THESIS I

There was once, we know, an automaton constructed in such a way that it could respond to every move by a chess player with a countermove that would ensure the winning of the game. A puppet wearing Turkish attire and with a hookah in its mouth sat before a chessboard placed on a large table. A system of mirrors created the illusion that this table was transparent on all sides. Actually, a hunchbacked dwarf – a master at chess – sat inside and guided the puppet's hand by means of strings. One can imagine a philosophic counterpart to this apparatus. The puppet, called 'historical materialism', is to win all the time. It can easily be a match for anyone if it enlists the services of theology, which today, as we know, is small and ugly and has to keep out of sight.

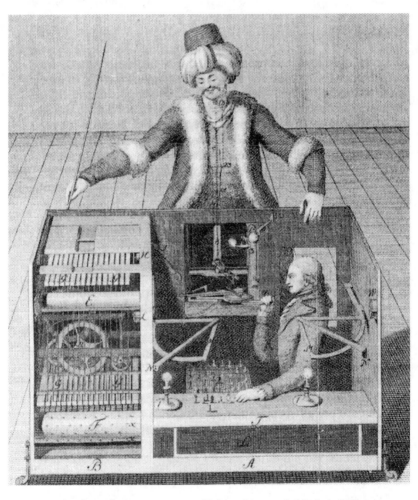

The chess-playing automaton of Johann Nepomuk Maelzel, 1769.

From the very outset, Thesis I announces one of the central themes of the text as a whole: the paradoxical combination of materialism and theology. To explain this, Benjamin creates an ironic allegory. Let us attempt to decipher the meaning of the elements that make it up.

First, the automaton: this is a puppet or marionette 'called "historical materialism" '. The use of quotation marks and the way this is phrased suggest that this automaton is not 'true' historical materialism, but something that is *given* that name. By whom, we ask. And the answer must be the chief spokesmen of Marxism in his period, that is to say the ideologues of the Second and Third Internationals. In Benjamin's view, historical materialism actually becomes in their hands a method that perceives history as akin to a machine leading 'automatically' to the triumph of socialism. For this mechanical materialism, the development of the productive forces, economic progress, the 'laws of history' lead necessarily to the last crisis of capitalism and the victory of the proletariat (Communist version) or to the reforms that will gradually transform society (Social Democratic version). Now this automaton, this manikin, this mechanical doll is not capable of 'winning the game'. 'Winning the game' here has a double meaning:

1. correctly interpreting history, struggling against the oppressors' view of history;
2. defeating the historic enemy itself, the ruling classes. In 1940, this meant Fascism.

For Benjamin, the two meanings are closely linked in the indissoluble unity of theory and practice: without a correct interpretation of history, it is difficult, if not impossible, to fight Fascism effectively. The defeat of the Marxist labour movement – in Germany, Austria, Spain and France – in the face of Fascism demonstrates the incapability of this soulless puppet, this insensate automaton, to 'win the game' – a game in which the future of humanity is at stake.

To win, historical materialism needs the help of theology: this is the little dwarf hidden in the machine. The allegory is, as we know, inspired by one of Edgar Allan Poe's stories, translated into French by Baudelaire and well known to Benjamin: namely, 'Maelzel's Chess Player'. It concerns a chess-playing automaton presented in 1769 to the Viennese Court by Baron Wolfgang von Kempelen, which was to end up, after its various travels, in the United States, being toured around the country by a Viennese inventor-cum-entrepreneur, Johann Nepomuk Maelzel. Poe describes this automaton as a figure 'habited as a Turk', which holds a pipe 'in the left hand' and which, if it were a machine, 'would always win' games of chess. One of the explanatory hypotheses discussed by Poe is that a 'dwarf actuated the machine', having previously concealed himself within it. The similarity – almost word for word – with Thesis I is clear.[12]

In our view, the relationship between Poe's text and Benjamin's thesis is not merely anecdotal. The philosophical conclusion of 'Maelzel's Chess-Player' is as follows: 'It is quite certain that the operations of the Automaton are regulated by mind, and by nothing else.' Poe's 'mind' becomes, in Benjamin's thesis, theology or, in other words, the messianic spirit, without which historical materialism cannot 'win the game' and the revolution cannot triumph.

It seems to us that Rolf Tiedemann is mistaken when, in his last – otherwise very interesting – book, he writes as follows: 'The theological dwarf is also dead, since he has become a component of a dead machine. The whole of the automaton is dead, and perhaps already represents the field of death and ruin of the ninth thesis.'[13] If the whole apparatus, dwarf included, is dead and ruined, how can he win the game against the opponent? What the thesis suggests is precisely the opposite: thanks to the vivifying action of the dwarf, the whole becomes alive and active . . .

The little dwarf, or the hunchbacked dwarf, as soul, as *spiritus rector* of an inanimate structure, is a typical theme of Romantic literature. Let us recall the Quasimodo of Hugo's *Notre Dame de Paris*:

> And the cathedral did indeed seem a docile and obedient creature beneath his hand . . . it was possessed and filled with Quasimodo, as with a familiar spirit . . . Egypt would have taken him for the god of this temple; the Middle Ages believed him to be its demon: he was in fact its soul.

Benjamin was fascinated by this theme: in his short story 'Rastelli's Tale' he presents a dwarf carefully concealed in a master juggler's ball and performing 'wonders' by 'work[ing] the compression springs in the interior of the ball'.[14]

Theology, like the dwarf in the allegory, can act today only in a concealed fashion in the interior of historical materialism. In a rationalist and unbelieving age, it is 'wizened and disreputable' (to quote Benjamin's French translation) and has to hide itself away . . . Curiously, Benjamin does not seem to conform to this rule since, in his 'Theses', theology is plainly visible. Perhaps, indeed, it is merely advice to the readers of the document: use theology, but do not show it. Or, alternatively, since the text was not intended for publication, it was not necessary to conceal the hunchbacked dwarf from the public gaze. In any event, the reasoning is analogous to that in a note to *The Arcades Project,* which Benjamin had incorporated into the so-called 'Paralipomena' to the theses: 'My thinking is related to theology as blotting pad is related to ink. It is saturated with it. Were one to go by the blotter, however, nothing of what is written would remain.'[15] Once again, the image of a determining – but invisible – presence of theology at the heart of 'profane' thought. The image is, moreover, somewhat curious. In fact, as those who used this now obsolete item of equipment know, traces of what was written in ink always remained on the surface of the blotter . . .

What does 'theology' mean for Benjamin? This will become clearer as we examine the 'Theses', but the term refers to two fundamental concepts: remembrance (*Eingedenken*) and messianic redemption (*Erlösung*). As we shall see, the two are essential components of the new 'concept of history' which the 'Theses' construct.

How, then, are we to interpret the relationship between theology and materialism? This question is presented in an eminently paradoxical way in the allegory: first, the theological dwarf appears as the master of the automaton, which he uses as an instrument; at the end, however, the dwarf is said to be 'in the service of' the automaton. What does this reversal mean? One possible hypothesis is that Benjamin wishes to show the dialectical complementarity between the two: theology and historical materialism are at times the master and at times the servant; they are both the master and the servant of each other, they need each other.

We must take seriously the idea that theology is 'in the service' of materialism – a formulation which reverses the traditional scholastic definition of philosophy as *ancilla theologiae* (servant of theology). Theology for Benjamin is not a goal in itself; its aim is not the ineffable contemplation of eternal verities, nor, even less, reflection on the nature of the divine Being, as might be thought from its etymology: it is in the service of the struggle of the oppressed. More precisely, it must serve to re-establish the explosive, messianic, revolutionary force of historical materialism – reduced to a wretched automaton by its epigones. The historical materialism to which Benjamin subscribes in the following theses is that which results from this vivification, this spiritual activation by theology.

According to Gerhard Kaiser, in the 'Theses' Benjamin 'theologizes Marxism. True historical materialism is true theology . . . His philosophy of history is a theology of history.' This type of interpretation destroys the delicate balance between the two components, reducing the one to the other. Any unilateral reductionism – in either direction – is incapable of accounting for the dialectic between theology and materialism and their need of each other.

In the opposite direction, Krista Greffrath thinks 'the theology of the "Theses" is an *auxiliary construction* . . . needed to wrest the tradition of the past from the hands of those who currently manage it'. This interpretation is in danger of presenting too contingent and instrumental a view of theology, when in reality it was an essential dimension of Benjamin's thinking from his earliest writings in 1913.

Lastly, Heinz-Dieter Kittsteiner believes he can see a sort of distinction of functions between the puppet and the dwarf: 'The historical materialist confronts the present as a Marxist, the past as a theologian of remembrance.' Now, this division of labour in no way corresponds to Benjamin's ideas: for him Marxism is as necessary to the understanding of the past as theology is for present and future action . . .'[16]

The idea of combining theology and Marxism is one of Benjamin's theses that has aroused the greatest incomprehension and perplexity. Yet, a few decades later, what in 1940 was merely an intuition was to become a historical phenomenon of the greatest importance in the form of Latin American liberation theology. This corpus of writings – by authors with impressive philosophical backgrounds, such as Gustavo Gutierrez, Hugo Assmann, Enrique Dussel, Leonardo Boff and many others – articulating Marxism to theology in a systematic way, played its part in changing the history of Latin America. Millions of Christians inspired by this theology that is present among the grassroots communities and in popular pastoral letters, played a key role in the Sandinista revolution in Nicaragua (1979), in the upsurge of guerrilla warfare in central America (El Salvador, Guatemala), in the formation of the new Brazilian workers' and peasants' movement – the Workers' Party (PT) and the Landless Movement (MST) – and even in the birth of the indigenous people's struggles in the Chiapas. In fact, most of the rebel social and political movements in Latin America in the last thirty years have been connected, to some degree, with liberation theology.[17]

This is, admittedly, different in many respects from the 'theology of revolution' sketched out by Benjamin – who is, indeed, unknown to the Latin American theologians. In this case, it was theology that had become an ossified puppet and it was the introduction of – a not necessarily concealed – Marxism that revitalized it. Furthermore, the theology in question is Christian, not Jewish, even if the messianic/prophetic dimension is present and the liberation theologians stress the 'Hebrew' character of early Christianity and the continuity between that Christianity and the spirit of the Old Testament. Lastly, the Latin American context is very different from that of inter-war Europe. Nonetheless, the combination of theology and Marxism the Jewish intellectual dreamed of has turned out, in the light of historical experience, to be not merely possible and fruitful, but a bearer of revolutionary change.

Thesis II

'It is one of the most noteworthy peculiarities of the human heart,' writes Lotze, 'that so much selfishness in individuals coexists with the general lack of envy which every present day feels towards its future.' This observation indicates that the image of happiness we cherish is thoroughly coloured by the time to which the course of our own existence has assigned us. There is happiness – such as could arouse envy in us – only in the air we have breathed, among people we could have talked to, women who could have given themselves to us. In other words, the idea of happiness is indissolubly bound up with the idea of redemption. The same applies to the idea of the past, which is the concern of history. The past carries with it a secret index by which it is referred to redemption. Doesn't a breath of the air that pervaded earlier

days caress us as well? In the voices we hear, isn't there an echo of now silent ones? Don't the women we court have sisters they no longer recognize? If so, then there is a secret agreement between past generations and the present one. Then our coming was expected on earth. Then, like every generation that preceded us, we have been endowed with a weak messianic power, a power on which the past has a claim. Such a claim cannot be settled cheaply. The historical materialist is aware of this.

Thesis II introduces one of the document's main theological concepts: *Erlösung*, which is correctly translated here as redemption.[18] Benjamin first situates this in the sphere of the individual: his personal happiness implies the redemption of his own past, the fulfilment of what could have been, but was not. According to the variant of this thesis in *The Arcades Project*, this happiness (*Glück*) implies reparation for the despair and desolation (*Trostlosigkeit, Verlassenheit*) of the past. The redemption of the past is nothing other than this fulfilment and this reparation according to the image of happiness held by each individual and generation.[19]

Thesis II moves imperceptibly from individual redemption to collective reparation on the terrain of history. To understand its argument, we must turn to *The Arcades Project*, which contains various quotations from Lotze, an author who was undoubtedly an important reference for Benjamin's thinking in the 'Theses'.

The German philosopher Hermann Lotze (1817–1881), long forgotten today, belongs to an Idealist metaphysical school close to Leibnizian monadism. His work *Mikrokosmus* expresses an ethical, religious philosophy of history tinged with melancholy, which attracted Benjamin's attention in the late 1930s. In a letter to Horkheimer of 24 January 1939 – a few months before the 'Theses' were composed – he says he has found unexpected support in Lotze's work for his reflections – already outlined in his article on Fuchs in 1938 – on the need to 'set limits to the use of the concept of progress in history'.[20]

According to extracts from *Mikrokosmus* cited by Benjamin in *The Arcades Project*, there is no progress if the souls that have suffered are not entitled to happiness (*Glück*) and fulfilment/completion (*Vollkommenheit*). Lotze rejects, then, the conceptions of history that are contemptuous of the demands (*Ansprüche*) of past ages and that regard the travails of past generations as irrevocably wasted. Progress has also to be achieved for past generations, in a mysterious (*geheimnisvolle*) way.[21]

We find these ideas almost word for word in Thesis II, which conceives redemption from the very first as historical remembrance of the victims of the past. Apart from Lotze's book, Benjamin also very probably draws his inspiration here from some remarks made by Horkheimer in an article on Bergson published in the *Zeitschrift für Sozialforschung* in 1934:

> What has happened to the human beings who have fallen no future can repair. They will never be called to be made happy for all eternity . . . Amid this immense indifference, human consciousness alone can become the site where the injustice suffered can be abolished [*aufgehoben*], the only agency that does not give in to it . . . Now that faith in eternity is necessarily breaking down, historiography [*Historie*] is the only court of appeal [*Gehör*] that present humanity, itself transient, can offer to the protests [*Anklagen*] which come from the past.[22]

The idea of an *Aufhebung* of past injustice through historical consciousness corresponds perfectly with Benjamin's intentions, but he gives it a theological dimension that Horkheimer no longer finds acceptable.

In a letter to Benjamin of 16 March 1937, Horkheimer returns to this problematic, but he does so mainly to criticize the 'idealist' character of a conception of history as being in a state of 'lack of closure' (*Unabgeschlossenheit*). 'Past injustice has occurred and is completed. The slain are really slain . . . If one takes the lack of closure entirely seriously, one has to believe in the Last Judgement . . .'[23] Benjamin accorded great importance to this letter, which he records in *The Arcades Project*, but he does not share his correspondent's strictly scientific, materialistic stance. He assigns a redemptive theological quality to remembrance, which is capable, in his view, of 'making into something incomplete' the apparently 'complete' suffering of the victims of the past. 'This is theology; but in remembrance (*Eingedenken*) we have an experience that forbids us from conceiving of history as fundamentally atheological, little as it may be granted us to try to write it with immediately theological concepts.'[24] Remembrance is, then, one of the tasks of the theological dwarf hidden in materialism, who must not show himself too 'directly'.

This discussion must not blind us to Benjamin's debt to Horkheimer's conceptions – particularly those laid out in his first book, *Dawn and Decline*. In that work, doubtless the most revolutionary he wrote, which was published in 1934 under the pseudonym Heinrich Regius, Horkheimer wrote:

> When you are at the lowest ebb, exposed to an eternity of torment inflicted upon you by other human beings, you cherish, as a dream of deliverance, the idea that a being will come who will stand in the light and bring truth and justice for you. You do not even need this to happen in your lifetime, nor in the lifetime of those who are torturing you to death, but one day, whenever it comes, all will nonetheless be repaired . . . It is bitter to be misunderstood and to die in obscurity. It is to the honour of historical research that it projects light into that obscurity.[25]

The affinity with Benjamin's theses is striking.

However, neither the remembrance and contemplation in consciousness of past injustices nor historical research are sufficient in Benjamin's eyes. For redemption to take place, there must be reparation – in Hebrew, *tikkun*[26] – for the suffering and grief inflicted on the defeated generations, and the accomplishment of the objectives they struggled for and failed to attain.

As is the case throughout the 'Theses', redemption may be understood here simultaneously in a theological and a secular sense. In the latter sense, it means – as we shall see become apparent in the following theses – the emancipation of the oppressed. The defeated of June 1848 – to mention an example that is very much present in *The Arcades Project* (but also in Marx's historical work) – await from us not just the remembrance of their suffering, but reparation for past injustices and the achievement of their social utopia. A secret pact binds us to them and we cannot easily throw off the demand they make upon us if we wish to remain faithful to historical materialism – that is to say, to a vision of history as a permanent struggle between the oppressed and the oppressors.

Messianic/revolutionary redemption is a task assigned to us by past generations. There is no Messiah sent from Heaven: we are ourselves the Messiah; each generation possesses a small portion of messianic power, which it must strive to exert.

The hypothesis, heretical from the standpoint of orthodox Judaism, of a 'messianic force' (*messianische Kraft*) attributed to humans is present also in other Central European Jewish thinkers, such as Martin Buber.[27] But, whereas for Buber what is involved is an auxiliary force that enables us to cooperate with God in the work of redemption, this duality seems to be abolished – in the sense of *aufgehoben* – in Benjamin. God is absent, and the messianic task falls wholly to the generations of human beings. The only possible Messiah is a collective one: it is humanity itself or, more precisely, as we shall see below, oppressed humanity. It is not a question of waiting for the Messiah, or calculating the day of his arrival – as among the cabbalists or the other Jewish mystics practising *gematria* – but of acting collectively. Redemption is a self-redemption and one can find the secular equivalent of this in Marx: men make their own history, the emancipation of the workers will be the task of the workers themselves.

What distinguishes Benjamin from Marx, however, is not just the theological dimension, but also the extent of the demand coming from the past: there will be no redemption for the present generation if it makes light of this claim (*Anspruch*) of the victims of history.[28]

Why is this messianic power *weak* (*schwach*)? As Giorgio Agamben has suggested, we might see this as a reference to the preaching of Christ according to St Paul in 2 Cor. 12: 9: for the Messiah 'my strength is made perfect in weakness'[29] (in Luther's translation: '*mein Kraft ist in den schwachen mechtig*').[30] But the expression also – probably – has a present political signification: the melancholy conclusion Benjamin draws from the past and present failures of the struggle for emancipation. Redemption is anything but assured; it is merely a slim possibility, which one has to know how to grasp.

Like the whole of the document, Thesis II is oriented towards both the past – history, remembrance – and the present: redemptive action. According to Jürgen Habermas, the rights the past claims over our messianic power 'can be respected only on condition that we constantly renew the critical effort of the gaze history directs onto a past calling for deliverance'.[31] The remark is legitimate, but too restrictive. Messianic power is not solely contemplative – the 'gaze history directs onto a past'. It is also active: redemption is a revolutionary task that is performed in the present. It is not merely a question of memory, but, as Thesis I reminds us, of winning a game against a powerful and dangerous opponent. 'Our coming was expected on earth' to rescue the defeated from oblivion, but also to continue and, if possible, complete their struggle for emancipation.

If Jewish prophecy is both a reminder of a promise and a call for a radical transformation, in Benjamin the violence of the prophetic tradition and the radicalism of Marxist critique meet in the demand for a salvation that is not mere restitution of the past, but also active transformation of the present.[32]

Theodor Adorno refers to Thesis II in an article that is Benjaminian in inspiration, entitled 'Progress' (1962), but he interprets it strangely, curiously reversing his friend's argument: 'In Benjamin progress obtains legitimation in the doctrine that the idea of the happiness of unborn generations – without which one cannot speak of progress – inalienably includes the idea of redemption.'[33] For Benjamin, it is not unborn generations that are at issue – we shall see later that he explicitly rejects the 'classical' progressive doctrine of fighting for generations yet to come – but those of the past and the present.

THESIS III

The chronicler who narrates events without distinguishing between major and minor ones acts in accord with the following truth: nothing that has ever happened should be regarded as lost to history. Of course, only a redeemed mankind is granted the fullness of its past – which is to say, only for a redeemed mankind has its past become citable in all its moments. Each moment it has lived becomes a citation à l'ordre du jour. *And that day is Judgement Day.*

There is a direct link between this thesis and the preceding one: it is a symmetrical and complementary inversion of it. The past awaits its redemption from us, and only a saved humanity can 'fully assume' the past. Once again, remembrance is at the heart of the theological relation to the past, and of the very definition of *Erlösung*. Redemption requires the integral remembrance of the past, without distinguishing between 'major' and 'minor' events or individuals. So long as the sufferings of a single human being are forgotten there can be no deliverance. It is doubtless a question here of what the preparatory notes, the so-called 'Paralipomena', refer to as the universal history of the messianic world, of the world of integral actuality.[34]

The example of the chronicler to illustrate this demand may seem ill-chosen: is he not the paradigmatic example of the person who writes history from the viewpoint of the winners, of the kings, princes and emperors? But Benjamin seems to wish deliberately to ignore this aspect: he chooses the chronicler because the chronicler represents the 'integral' history he is calling for: a history that excludes no detail, no event, however insignificant, and for which nothing is 'lost'. The Russian writer Leskov, Franz Kafka and Anna Seghers are, in his view, modern figures of the chronicler understood in this way.

Irving Wohlfarth, one of the most insightful readers of Benjamin's work, rightly stresses that the chronicler anticipates the Last Judgement which, like him, rejects any form of discrimination – a view that reminds us somewhat of the doctrine, mentioned by Benjamin in his essay on Leskov, of certain schools of thought within the Orthodox Church which hold that all souls go to Paradise.[35] And Benjamin does indeed, in 'The Storyteller' (1936), mention Leskov's sympathy for Origen's speculations regarding *apokatastasis*, the ultimate salvation of all souls without exception.[36] The redemption, the Last Judgement of Thesis III, is, then, an *apokatastasis* in the sense that every past victim, every attempt at emancipation, however humble and 'minor', will be rescued from oblivion and 'mentioned in dispatches' (*citée à l'ordre du jour*), that is to say recognized, honoured and remembered.

But *apokatastasis* means also, literally, the return of all things to their original state – in the Gospels, the re-establishment of Paradise by the Messiah. It is the idea of the *Wiederbringung aller Dinge* (return of all things) or the *versöhnende Rückkehr am Ende der Dinge* (reconciled return to the end of all things) Lotze dreamed of in *Mikrokosmus*:[37] the secret or mysterious form by which progress could incorporate the spirits of the ancestors. In other words, it is a question of the *restitutio ad integrum* or *restitutio omnium* Benjamin was already writing of in his 'Theological-Political Fragment' of 1921. The Jewish, messianic and cabbalistic equivalent of the Christian *apokatastasis* is, as Scholem argues in his article 'Kabbala' in the *Encyclopaedia Judaica* (1932), *tikkun*: redemption as the return of all things to their primal state.[38] Benjamin had been deeply impressed by this piece by Scholem, as he records in a letter of 15 January

1933 to his friend: 'the rays of your article' forced their way down into 'the abyss of my ignorance in this area'.[39] In the French translation of Thesis III made by Benjamin himself, he writes of '*l'humanité restituée, sauvée, rétablie*' – three terms that relate to *apokatastasis* and *tikkun*.

From Origen, through Gregory of Nyssa, John Scotus Eriugena and the Anabaptists to Schleiermacher, the concept of *apokatastasis* has a dual significance: the *restitutio* of the past is, at the same time, a *novum*. This is exactly what Scholem writes of the Jewish messianic tradition: it is animated both by the desire for the restoration of the original state of things and by a utopian vision of the future, in a kind of mutual illumination.[40]

The utopian-revolutionary dimension of *apokatastasis* is not explicitly present in Thesis III, but it is suggested in a paragraph in *The Arcades Project*. Benjamin quotes a critique of the Surrealists by Emmanuel Berl: 'Instead of following the course of the modern world', Berl argues, the Surrealists tried to relocate themselves to 'a moment anterior even to the development of Marxism: the period of the 1820s, 30s and 40s – a clear reference to the utopian socialists and/or Blanqui. Now, for the author of *The Arcades Project*, this refusal to follow 'the course of the modern world' – an expression that could only arouse contempt – is precisely one of the great virtues of Surrealism, a movement inspired by 'the will to apocatastasis . . . the resolve to gather again, in revolutionary action and in revolutionary thinking, precisely the elements of the "too early" and the "too late" of the first beginning and the final decay'.[41] As remembrance of forgotten battles and the rescue of endeavours against the grain, the *apokatastasis* of the 'lost' utopian moments of socialism is not a contemplative operation on the part of the Surrealists: it is in the service of the revolutionary thought and practice of the present, here and now – *jetzt*!

There is no question, for Benjamin, of replacing Marx with utopian socialism: his many references to historical materialism show this sufficiently. But it is a question of enriching revolutionary culture with all the aspects of the past that bear utopian hope within them: Marxism has no meaning if it is not, also, the heir to – and executor of – many centuries of emancipatory dreams and struggles.

Thesis IV

Seek for food and clothing first, then
shall the Kingdom of God be granted to you.
G. W. F. Hegel, 1807

Class struggle, which for a historian schooled in Marx is always in evidence, is a fight for the crude and material things without which no refined and spiritual things could exist. But these latter things, which are present in class struggle, are not present as a vision of spoils that fall to the victor. They are alive in this struggle as confidence, courage, humour, cunning and fortitude, and have effects that reach far back into the past. They constantly call into question every victory, past and present, of the rulers. As flowers turn towards the sun, what has been strives to turn – by dint of a secret heliotropism – towards that sun which is rising in the sky of history. The historical materialist must be aware of this most inconspicuous of all transformations.

Let us begin with the Hegel text, an ironic inversion of the well-known passage in the Christian gospels: it illustrates to perfection Benjamin's method of quotation, which consists in despoiling the author of his text the way a highwayman takes jewels from a rich traveller. The passage is literally wrenched from its context: Hegel, the great Idealist philosopher, testifies to the most elementary materialism.

At the same time, the epigraph connects Thesis IV to the two preceding theses. That is to say, it connects them to the theme of redemption: no salvation without revolutionary transformations of material life. The concept of the Kingdom of God that appears here is somewhat reminiscent of that of Thomas Münzer, as Friedrich Engels presents him in *The Peasant War in Germany* (1850): 'By the kingdom of God Münzer meant a society without class differences, private property and a state authority independent of, and foreign to, the members of society.'[42] With the slight difference that Benjamin would not go so far as so fully to secularize the theological significance of the concept.

The historical materialism, the being 'schooled in Marx' that is referred to here is, of course, reinterpreted by Benjamin in his own terms: it is a heterodox, heretical, idiosyncratic, uncategorizable version. In certain respects Benjamin is close here to Brecht: like him, he insists on the priority of 'crude and material things'. 'Food first, then morality', sing the characters in *The Threepenny Opera*. However, unlike his friend, Benjamin accords crucial importance to spiritual and moral forces in the class struggle: faith [*foi*] – Benjamin's translation of the word *Zuversicht* [43] – courage and perseverance. The list of spiritual qualities includes two others that are perfectly 'Brechtian': humour and, above all, the *cunning* of the oppressed.

There is, then, in Benjamin a dialectic of the material and the spiritual in the class struggle that goes beyond the rather mechanistic model of infrastructure and superstructure: the stakes in the struggle are material, but the motivation of the social actors is spiritual. If it were not driven by certain moral qualities, the dominated class could not fight for its liberation.

Let us try to pin down Benjamin's Marxism more precisely. The most essential concept of historical materialism for him is not abstract philosophical materialism: it is *class struggle*. It is that struggle that 'is constantly present to the historian schooled by the thought of Karl Marx' (*ne cesse d'être présent à l'historien formé par la pensée de Karl Marx* – this is Benjamin's own French translation). And it is that struggle too which enables us to understand the present, past and future, as well as the secret bond between them. It is the place where theory and praxis coincide – and we know it is that coincidence which initially drew Benjamin to Marxism when he read Lukács's *History and Class Consciousness* in 1924. [44]

Though almost all Marxists make reference to the class struggle, few devote such passionate, intense and exclusive attention to it as Walter Benjamin. What interests him in the past is not the development of the productive forces, the contradiction between the forces and relations of production, forms of property or state forms or the development of modes of production – essential themes of Marx's work – but the life and death struggle between oppressors and oppressed, exploiters and exploited, dominators and dominated.

History thus appears to him as a succession of victories by the powerful. The power of a ruling class is not the mere product of its economic and political force, or of the distribution of property, or of the transformations of the productive system: it always implies a historic triumph in the battle against the subordinate classes. Against the evolutionary view of history as an accumulation of 'gains', as 'progress' towards ever more freedom, rationality or civilization, he sees it 'from below', from the standpoint of the defeated, as a series of victories of the ruling classes. His formulation is quite clearly also distinct from Marx and Engels's famous statement in the *Communist Manifesto* which stresses, rather, the victory of the revolutionary classes over the course of history − save in the exceptional case of 'the common ruin of the contending classes'.[45]

However, each new battle on the part of the oppressed puts in question not only present domination, but also those past victories. The *forces spirituelles* (Benjamin's own translation into French) of the current struggle '*rayonnent*' [shine forth] into the distant past, into '*la nuit des temps*' [the mists − literally, the night − of time]. The past is lit by the light of today's battles, by the sun rising in the firmament of history. The metaphor of the sun was a traditional image of the German labour movement: '*Brüder, zu Sonne, zur Freiheit*' [Brothers, to sun, to freedom], proclaimed the old anthem of the Social Democratic Party. But this was a reference to the sun of the future that illumines the present. Here it is thanks to the sun of the present that the meaning of the past is transformed for us. Thus, as in the example cited above, Thomas Münzer and the peasant wars of the sixteenth century are reinterpreted by Friedrich Engels − and later by Ernst Bloch − in the light of the battles of the modern workers' movement.[46]

Current struggles cast into question the historical victories of the oppressors because they undermine the legitimacy of the power of the ruling classes, past and present. Benjamin is here explicitly taking a stand against a certain evolutionary conception of Marxism − already present in certain passages in Marx's writings (among others, the *Communist Manifesto* and the articles on India of the 1850s) − that justifies the victories of the bourgeoisie in the past by the laws of history, the need to develop the productive forces or the unripe character of the conditions for social emancipation.

The relation between today and yesterday is not a unilateral one: in an eminently dialectical process, the present illumines the past and the illumined past becomes a force in the present. Old battles are turned 'toward the rising sun', but they fuel the class consciousness of those who are rising up today, once they are touched by its rays. The 'sun' here is not, as in the tradition of the 'progressive' Left, the symbol of the necessary, inevitable and 'natural' advent of a new world, but a symbol of the struggle itself and the utopian vision it inspires.[47]

Thesis V

The true image of the past flits by. The past can be seized only as an image which flashes up at the moment of its recognizability and is never seen again. 'The truth will not run away from us': this statement by Gottfried Keller indicates exactly that point in historicism's image of history where the image is pierced by historical materialism. For it is an irretrievable image of the past which threatens to disappear in any present that does not recognize itself as intended in that image.

A first version of Thesis V can already be found in the 1936 essay on Fuchs: against the contemplative attitude of the traditional historian, Benjamin stresses the active engagement of the historical materialist. His objective is to discover the critical constellation formed by a particular fragment of the past with a particular moment of the present. The political and active dimension of this relation to the past is made explicit in one of the paralipomena to the theses: 'This concept [of the present] creates a connection between the writing of history and politics that is identical to the theological connection between remembrance and redemption. This present is expressed in images that may be called dialectical. They represent a salutary intervention [*rettenden Einfall*] of humanity.'[48] We find here again the paradoxical idea – though one that is essential to Benjamin's intellectual approach – of a sort of identity between certain theological concepts and their secular, revolutionary equivalents. Moreover, one should not lose sight of the fact that the 'salutary intervention' is aimed as much at the past as at the present: history and politics, remembrance and redemption are inseparable.

The concept of 'dialectics' is borrowed here by Benjamin from Hegelo-Marxist phraseology: he is attempting to account for the nature of a 'salutary image' that seeks to achieve the sublation – *Aufhebung* – of the contradictions between past and present, theory and practice.

An example which does not come from Benjamin may enable us to cast light on Thesis V. The dialectical image of 'permanent revolution' formulated by Trotsky in 1905–6 was based on the perception of a critical constellation between the Russian revolution of 1905 and the Paris Commune of 1871. But this fleeting image that momentarily 'flit[ted] by' the historian/political actor was lost. The Russian labour movement of the time did not recognize itself as implicated by the Paris Commune: both the Mensheviks and the Bolsheviks – see Lenin's writings of 1905 – explicitly rejected the reference to the Commune, which was criticized for having 'confused the democratic with the proletarian revolution'.[49] The joyous message the historian/militant brought 'breathless' from the past fell on deaf ears. It would be a dozen more years before, with Lenin's 'April Theses' – which draw inspiration from the model of the Commune of 1871 – a new constellation could emerge, this time successfully.

An illuminating comment by Jeanne-Marie Gagnebin on Benjamin's 'open history' applies very exactly to Thesis V: she writes that Benjamin shared with Proust

> the concern to rescue the past in the present, thanks to the perception of a resemblance that transforms them both: it transforms the past because the past takes on a new form, which could have disappeared into oblivion; it transforms the present because the present reveals itself as being the possible fulfilment of that earlier promise – a promise which could have been lost for all time, which can still be lost if it is not discovered and inscribed in the lineaments of the present.[50]

Krista Greffrath observes that this thesis in fact signifies the most radical historicization of historical truth: the true image of the past is itself subject to the historical process. So long as history does not come to a stop, the last word on the past cannot be pronounced. This interpretation is interesting, but too restrictive: it limits *Rettung* to the historiographical domain and forgets that of political intervention. Now, as we have seen, for Benjamin the two are strictly inseparable.[51]

One objection to this 'political' conception of the past deserves to be examined here: does this not run the risk of leading to an 'Orwellian' rewriting of the past, in terms of the present political needs of a totalitarian apparatus or state – as has already been abundantly demonstrated by Stalinist practice in the late 1930s in the USSR? Benjamin's argument is, however, radically distinct from that totalitarian model in several respects:

1. there is never in Benjamin a claim to a monopoly of historical truth, and even less to impose such a truth on the whole of society;
2. whereas the Stalinist apparatus claimed to possess a changeless, final truth, fixed once and for all, denying any past or future change, Benjamin speaks of a fleeting, fragile image that 'flits by';
3. there is no place in Benjamin for a state or state apparatus exerting ideological hegemony: the historian is an *individual* who always runs the risk of not being understood by his times.

Thesis VI

Articulating the past historically does not mean recognizing it 'the way it really was'. It means appropriating a memory as it flashes up in a moment of danger. Historical materialism wishes to hold fast that image of the past which unexpectedly appears to the historical subject in a moment of danger. The danger threatens both the content of the tradition and those who inherit it. For both, it is one and the same thing: the danger of becoming a tool of the ruling classes. Every age must strive anew to wrest tradition away from the conformism that is working to overpower it. The Messiah comes not only as the redeemer; he comes as the victor over the Antichrist. The only historian capable of fanning the spark of hope in the past is the one who is firmly convinced that even the dead *will not be safe from the enemy if he is victorious. And this enemy has never ceased to be victorious.*

The thesis begins by rejecting the historicist/positivist conception of history, represented by the famous phrase of Ranke, the conformist and conservative Prussian historian, which sees the task of the historian as being, quite simply, to represent the past 'the way it really was'. The alleged neutral historian, who has access directly to the 'real' facts, in reality only reinforces the view of the victors – the kings, popes and emperors (the preferred object of Ranke's historiography) of all ages.

Meissonnier, *The Barricade*.

The moment of danger for the historical subject – that is to say, the oppressed classes (and the historian who has chosen their side) – is the moment when the authentic image of the past emerges. Why? Probably because in that instant the comfortable, lazy vision of history as uninterrupted 'progress' dissolves. The danger of a current defeat sharpens the sensitivity to preceding ones, arouses interest in the battle fought by the defeated, and encourages a critical view of history. Benjamin is thinking perhaps of his own situation too: was it not the imminent danger in which he found himself in 1939–40 – arrest, internment, being handed over to the Gestapo by the Vichy authorities – that gave rise to the singular, if not indeed, unique view of the past that emerges from the 'Theses "On the Concept of History"'?

In the moment of danger, when the dialectical image 'flashes up' or 'flits by', the historian – or revolutionary – has to show presence of mind (*Geistesgegenwart*) to grasp this unique moment, this fleeting and precarious opportunity of salvation (*Rettung*) before it is too late.[52] Because this memory may, as Benjamin's French version of this thesis underscores, be precisely what 'saves him' (*le sauve*).[53]

The danger is twofold: of transforming both the history of the past – the tradition of the oppressed – and the current historical subject – the dominated classes, 'new heirs' to that tradition – into tools in the hands of the ruling classes. To wrest tradition away from the conformism that is working to overpower it is to restore to history – for example, the history of the French Revolutions of 1789 or 1848 – its dimension of subversion of the established order, which is toned down, obliterated or denied by the 'official' historians. It is only in this way that the historical materialist can 'fan the spark of hope in the past' – a spark which can ignite the powder keg *today*.

The revolutionary historian knows the victory of the present enemy threatens even the dead – not necessarily in the crude, primitive form of the Stuart Restoration, when Cromwell's remains were abused, but by the falsification or forgetting of their struggles. Now, 'this enemy has never ceased to be victorious': from the point of view of the oppressed, the past is not a gradual accumulation of conquests, as in 'progressive' historiography, but an interminable series of catastrophic defeats: the crushing of the slave rebellion against Rome, of the revolt of the Anabaptist peasants of the sixteenth century, of June 1848, of the Paris Commune and the Spartakist rising of 1919 in Berlin.

But it is not just a question of the past: in his French translation, Benjamin writes: '*A l'heure qu'il est, l'ennemi n'a pas encore fini de triompher*' [At the present time, the enemy is still continuing to triumph]. And in 1940, the time was 'midnight in the century', to borrow once again Serge's fine expression. The enemy's victories were monumental: the defeat of Republican Spain, the Nazi-Soviet Pact, the occupation of Europe by the Third Reich.

Benjamin knew well this present enemy: Fascism. For the oppressed, it represents the supreme danger, the greatest danger they have ever encountered in history: the second death of the victims of the past and the massacre of all the enemies of the regime. The falsification of the past on an unprecedented scale and the transformation of the popular masses into a tool of the ruling classes. Of course, in spite of his vocation as a Cassandra and his radical pessimism, Benjamin could not predict Auschwitz . . .

In the text of the lecture on Baudelaire delivered at Pontigny in May 1939 Benjamin observed that the crowds are today 'moulded by the hands of the dictators'. But he does not despair of 'glimpsing in these enslaved crowds cores of resistance – cores formed by the revolutionary masses of 1848 and the Communards'.[54] In other words, in a moment of supreme danger, a saving constellation presents itself, linking the present to the past. A past in which, in spite of everything, in the dark night of Fascism, there shines the star of hope, the messianic star of redemption – Franz Rosenzweig's *Stern der Erlösung* – the spark of the revolutionary uprising.

Now, writes Benjamin, 'the Messiah comes not only as the redeemer; he comes as the victor over the Antichrist.' Commenting on this passage, Tiedemann notes a startling paradox: 'Nowhere else does Benjamin speak so directly theologically as he does here, yet nowhere does he have such a materialist intention.' We have to see the Messiah as the proletarian class and the Antichrist as the ruling classes.[55]

The observation is apt, but we might, for more precision, add that the secular equivalent – the '*correspondant*' – of the Messiah today are the core groups of anti-Fascist resistance, the future revolutionary masses who are heirs to the tradition of June 1848 and April–May 1871. As for the Antichrist – a Christian *theologoumenon* which Benjamin does not hesitate to incorporate

into his explicitly Jewish-inspired messianic argument – his secular counterpart is undoubtedly Hitler's Third Reich.

In a 1938 review of a novel by Anna Seghers entitled *Die Rettung*, which
tells the story of one of the Communist resistance cells in Nazi Germany,
Benjamin writes that the Third Reich mimics socialism the way 'the coming
of the Antichrist . . . mimics the blessing promised by the coming of the
Messiah'.[56] For this striking parallel, Benjamin took his inspiration from the
writings of his friend the Swiss Protestant theological and revolutionary
socialist Fritz Lieb, who, as early as 1934, had defined Nazism as the modern
Antichrist. In a lecture of 1938, Lieb had expressed his hope of seeing the
Antichrist defeated in a last battle against the Jews that would bring the
appearance of the Messiah – the Christ – and the establishment of his
millennial kingdom.[57]

THESIS VII

Bedenkt das Dunkel und die grosse Kälte
In diesem Tale, das von Jammer schallt.

(Consider the darkness and the great cold
In this vale resounding with misery.)
Bertolt Brecht, 'Schlusschoral'
from *The Threepenny Opera*

Addressing himself to the historian who wishes to relive an era, Fustel de Coulanges
recommends that he blot out everything he knows about the later course of history. There
is no better way of characterizing the method which historical materialism has broken
with. It is a process of empathy. Its origin is indolence of the heart, that acedia *which*
despairs of appropriating the genuine historical image as it briefly flashes up. Among
medieval theologians, acedia *was regarded as the root cause of sadness. Flaubert, who*
was familiar with it, wrote: 'Peu de gens devineront combien il a fallu être triste
pour ressusciter Carthage!' *The nature of this sadness becomes clearer if we ask:*
With whom does historicism actually sympathize? The answer is inevitable: with the
victor. And all rulers are the heirs of prior conquerors. Hence, empathizing with the

victor invariably benefits the current rulers. The historical materialist knows what this means. Whoever has emerged victorious participates to this day in the triumphal procession in which current rulers step over those who are lying prostrate. According to traditional practice, the spoils are carried in the procession. They are called 'cultural treasures,' and a historical materialist views them with cautious detachment. For in every case, these treasures have a lineage which he cannot contemplate without horror. They owe their existence not only to the efforts of the great geniuses who created them, but also to the anonymous toil of others who lived in the same period. There is no document of culture which is not at the same time a document of barbarism. And just as such a document is never free of barbarism, so barbarism taints the manner in which it was transmitted from one hand to another. The historical materialist therefore dissociates himself from this process of transmission as far as possible. He regards it as his task to brush history against the grain.

The polemic against Fustel de Coulanges, the reactionary nineteenth-century French positivist historian,[58] continues and extends that of the earlier theses against Ranke and German historicism: the past can be understood only in the light of the present; its true image is fleeting and precarious; it 'flits by'. But Benjamin introduces a new concept here, that of *Einfühlung*, the closest equivalent to which is empathy, but which he himself translates into French not as '*empathie*', but as '*identification affective*'. He accuses historicism of identifying with the victor. Self-evidently, the term 'victor' does not refer here to common battles or wars, but to the 'class war' in which one of the sides, the ruling class, has constantly won out over the oppressed – from Spartacus the rebellious gladiator to Rosa Luxemburg's Spartakusbund, and from the Roman *Imperium* to Hitler's *Tertium Imperium* or Third Reich.

The origin of the empathy that identifies with the triumphal procession of the dominators is to be found, according to Benjamin, in *acedia*, a Latin term which denotes indolence of the heart, melancholia. Why? What is the relationship between *acedia* and *Einfühlung*? Thesis VII does not explain this in any way, but we can find the key to the problem in *The Origin of German Tragic Drama* (1925): *acedia* is the melancholy sense of the omnipotence of fate which removes all value from human activities. It leads, consequently, to total submission to the existing order of things. As profound, melancholy meditation, it feels attracted by the solemn majesty of the triumphal procession of the powerful. The melancholic, par excellence, dominated by indolence of the heart – *acedia* – is the courtier. Betrayal is his element, because his submission to destiny always makes him join the victor's camp.[59]

The modern equivalent of the Baroque courtier is the conformist historian. He too always chooses objective identification with the majestic triumphal procession of the powerful. The great historian Heinrich von Sybel, a disciple of Ranke, was not at all reluctant to proclaim that success is 'the supreme judge . . . and direct deciding factor' in the eyes of the historian. This attitude was not just the prerogative of German historiography: Benjamin here cites Fustel de Coulanges; he might also have mentioned Victor Cousin who, in his *Introduction to the History of Philosophy* of 1828, develops an impressive 'philosophy of the victors' which, with admirable elegance, links success with 'morality':

> I pardon victory as necessary and useful; I shall undertake now to pardon it as just, in the narrowest sense of the word; I shall undertake to demonstrate the morality of success. Ordinarily, success is seen merely as the triumph of force and a kind of sentimental sympathy attracts us to the defeated party. I hope that I have demonstrated that, since there always has to be a defeated party, and the victor is always the party who has to win, it must be proved that the victor not only serves civilization, but that he is better and more moral and it is for that reason he is the victor. If it were not thus, there would be a contradiction between morality and civilization, which is impossible, the two being merely two sides, two distinct but harmonious elements, of the same idea.[60]

It is against precisely this servile historicism that Benjamin is rebelling when he proposes to 'brush history against the grain'. Without doubt he takes his inspiration here from the early Nietzsche, the author of the second of the 'Untimely Observations', *On the Advantage and Disadvantage of History for Life* (1873), a work read, admired and quoted (including in the 'Theses') by Benjamin.

Nietzsche had nothing but scorn for the historians 'swimming and drowned in the flow of becoming', who practise 'naked admiration for success' and 'the idolatry of the factual' – in short, for the historian who always 'nods his "yes"', mechanically, like a Chinese to any power'. In his eyes, the devil is the true master of success and progress: virtue for the historian consists in 'swim[ming] against the historical waves' and knowing how to struggle against them.[61]

Benjamin entirely shared these sentiments and drew on them in his refusal to imitate those who brush '*le poil trop luisant*' [the over-glossy coat] of history – an ironic expression Benjamin uses in his French translation of Thesis VII – the right way about. The decisive difference between the two is that Nietzsche's critique is made in the name of the rebellious individual, the hero – and later the overman. That of Benjamin, by contrast, is in solidarity with those who have fallen beneath the wheels of those majestic, magnificent chariots called Civilization, Progress and Modernity.

Brushing history against the grain – a formula of tremendous historiographical and political significance – means, then, first of all, the refusal in one way or another to join the triumphal procession, which continues, even today, to ride roughshod over the bodies of those who are prostrate. One thinks of those Baroque allegories of triumph that depict princes riding on a magnificent imperial chariot, sometimes with prisoners and chests overflowing with gold and jewels in train; or of that other image – which Marx uses to describe capital – of Juggernaut, the Hindu divinity, seated on an immense chariot, beneath whose wheels are hurled the children that are to be sacrificed. But the old model that remains in the mind of all Jews is the Arch of Titus in Rome, which represents the triumphal procession of the Roman victors against the Jewish Revolt, bearing the treasures looted from the Temple of Jerusalem.[62]

As ever in Benjamin, the imperative of 'brush[ing] history against the grain' has a dual meaning:

1. *Historical*: this means going against the grain of the official version of history, setting the tradition of the oppressed against that version. From this point of view the historical continuity of the ruling classes can be seen as an enormous, single triumphal procession, occasionally interrupted by uprisings on the part of the subordinate classes;

2. *Political (and current)*: redemption/revolution will not occur in the mere natural course of things, by dint of the 'meaning of history' or inevitable progress. One has to struggle against the tide. Left to itself, or brushed *with* the grain, so to speak, history will produce only new wars, fresh catastrophes, novel forms of barbarism and oppression.

School of Mantegna, *The Triumph of Caesar*, fifteenth century.

We are back here with the revolutionary pessimism of Benjamin (who called in his article on *Surrealism* (1929) for the urgent organization of pessimism), which is equally as opposed to the melancholy fatalism of 'indolence of the heart' as it is to the optimistic fatalism of the official – Social Democratic or Communist – Left, confident in the 'inevitable' victory of the 'progressive forces'.

   Benjamin's thinking also roves over the barbaric reverse side of the brilliant, gilded medal of culture, that booty which passes from one victor to another like the seven-branched candelabra, the Jerusalem Temple Menorah, in the same *haut relief* on the Arch of Titus. Instead of contrasting

The Triumphal Arch of Titus, Roman Forum, AD 96.
Copperplate engraving, eighteenth century.

culture (or civilization) and barbarism as two mutually exclusive poles, or as different stages of historical evolution – two classic leitmotivs of Enlightenment philosophy – Benjamin presents them dialectically as a contradictory unity.

Triumphal arches are a notable example of monuments of culture that are at the same time, and indissociably, monuments of barbarism celebrating war and massacre. Benjamin's interest in this kind of architecture, its origins in ancient Rome, its political and ideological function, is attested by *The Arcades Project*.[63] In 'Berlin Childhood', we find a terrifying description of the *Siegessäule*, the Victory Column, which stresses the contrast between the grace of the statue of Victory that sits atop the monument and the dark frescoes of its lower part, representing – in the child's imagination – scenes in which 'multitudes . . . lashed by whirlwinds, encased in bloody tree stumps, or sealed in blocks of ice' suffer like the damned of Dante's *Inferno*, as drawn by Gustave Doré.[64] There is a striking parallel between this description and Brecht's poem that provides the epigraph to Thesis VII.

The dialectic between culture and barbarism applies also to many other prestigious works produced by the 'anonymous toil' of the oppressed – from the pyramids of Egypt, built by Hebrew slaves, to the Palais de l'Opéra erected, under Napoleon III, by the defeated workers of June

Gustave Doré, *The Lustful*. Illustration for Dante's *Inferno*, 1861.

Gustave Doré, *Cocytus* (detail). Illustration for Dante's *Inferno*, 1861.

1848. In this thesis we find the inverted image of a theme dear to
Nietzsche: the great works of art and civilization – the pyramids being
a prime example – can be produced only by subjecting the multitudes to
suffering and enslavement. For the philosopher of Sils-Maria, this was an
inevitable, necessary sacrifice.

Writing this text, Benjamin no doubt had in mind Brecht's ironic,
irreverent poem of 1935, 'Questions from a Worker who Reads':

> Who built Thebes of the seven gates?
> In the books you will find the names of kings.
> Did the kings haul up the lumps of rock?
> And Babylon many times demolished.
> Who raised it up so many times? . . .
>
> . . . Great Rome
> Is full of triumphal arches. Who erected them?
> Over whom
> Did the Caesars triumph? . . .
>
> Every page a victory.
> Who cooked the feast for the victors?
> Every ten years a great man.
> Who paid the bill?
>
> So many reports.
> So many questions.[65]

But Thesis VII has a more general significance: high culture could not exist in
its historical form without the anonymous labour of the direct producers –
slaves, peasants or workers – themselves excluded from the enjoyment of
cultural goods. These latter are, therefore, 'document[s] of barbarism' insofar
as they are the products of class injustice, social and political oppression and
inequality and because they are handed down by way of wars and massacres.
The 'cultural heritage' passed from Greece to Rome and thence to the
Church. From there it has fallen into the hands of the bourgeoisie, where it
has remained from the Renaissance to our own day. In each case, the ruling
elite appropriates the preceding culture either by conquest or other barbaric
means and integrates it into its system of social and ideological domination.

Culture and tradition thus become, as Benjamin emphasizes in his Thesis VI, 'a tool of the ruling classes'.

To brush cultural history *gegen den Strich* means, then, to view it from the standpoint of the defeated, the excluded, the pariahs. For example, the rich culture of the French Second Empire must be examined, as Benjamin does in *The Arcades Project*, by taking account of the defeat of the workers in June 1848 and the repression of the revolutionary movement (Blanqui!) over several decades to which that defeat led. Similarly, the glittering culture of Weimar must be seen in relation to the situation of the unemployed, the poor and the victims of inflation – as in *One-Way Street*. In other words, to quote one of the preparatory notes for the 'Theses', the history of culture 'has to be integrated into the history of the class struggle'.[66]

This does not mean that Benjamin advocated 'cultural populism': far from rejecting the works of 'high culture' as reactionary, he was of the opinion that many of them were overtly or covertly hostile to capitalist society. The point was, then, to recover the utopian or subversive moments hidden in the 'cultural' heritage, whether it be in the fantastic tales of Hoffmann, Baudelaire's poems or Leskov's stories. According to Richard Wolin, Benjamin in his last essays and in the 'Theses' 'no longer speaks of the *Aufhebung* of traditional bourgeois culture, an idea he entertained in "The Work of Art" essay and his commentaries on Brecht; rather it is the effort to preserve and render exotic the secret utopian potential embedded in traditional works of culture that Benjamin views as the preeminent task of materialist criticism'.[67] This is true inasmuch as this 'preservation' is dialectically linked to the destructive moment: it is only by breaking through the reified outer husk of official culture that the oppressed can take possession of this critical/utopian kernel.

Benjamin is concerned to safeguard the subversive, anti-bourgeois forms of culture, by seeking to prevent their being embalmed, neutralized, lauded and academicized (Baudelaire) by the cultural establishment. There is a fight to be had to prevent the ruling class from extinguishing the flames of past culture, and to preserve that culture from the conformism that threatens it (Thesis VI).[68]

We may illustrate the significance of the demand that history be 'brush[ed] . . . against the grain' with a recent Latin American example:

the celebration of the cinquecentennial of the discovery of the Americas (1492–1992). The cultural festivities organized by the state, the Church or by private initiative are fine examples of empathy with the victors of the sixteenth century, an *Einfühlung* which unfailingly redounds to the advantage of today's leaders, the local and multinational financial elites that have inherited the power of the old conquistadors.

To write history '*à contre-sens*' (the term Benjamin uses in his own French translation of the 'Theses') is to refuse any 'affective identification' with the official heroes of the cinquecentennial, the Iberian colonialists and the European powers who brought religion, culture and civilization to the 'savage' Indians. This means regarding every monument of colonial culture – the cathedrals of Mexico City or Lima, Cortez's palace at Cuernavaca – as being *also* a document of barbarism, a product of war, extermination and ruthless oppression.

For centuries, the 'official' history of the discovery, conquest and conversion of South America was not merely hegemonic, but practically the only version on the political and cultural scene. It was not until the Mexican Revolution of 1911 that this hegemony began to be contested. Diego

Diego Rivera, *The Capture of Cuernavaca*. Mural.
Cortez's Palace, Cuernavaca, Mexico, 1930.

Rivera's frescoes at Cortez's Palace in Cuernavaca (1930) mark a genuine turning point in the history of Latin American culture by their iconoclastic demystification of the conquistador and the artist's sympathy for the native warriors.[69] Fifty years later, *Open Veins of Latin America* (1981), the famous work by one of the continent's greatest essayists, the Uruguayan Eduardo Galeano, presents, in a powerful synthesis, the charge sheet of Iberian colonization from the point of view of the victims and their cultures, the Indians, the black slaves and the mestizos.

During the debate on the cinquecentennial, Galeano intervened in almost Benjaminian terms – I do not know if he has ever read the 1940 'Theses' – to call for 'the celebration of the defeated, not the victors' and 'the safeguarding of some of our oldest traditions', such as the communal way of life, because it is 'from its most ancient sources' that America can draw to find its 'freshest lifeblood': 'The past says things that concern the future.'[70]

While Spain, Europe and the USA were preparing to celebrate the coming of Christopher Columbus, a Latin American meeting held at Xelaju, Guatemala, one of the bastions of Maya culture, in October 1991 called for the commemoration of 'five centuries of black, Indian and popular resistance'. The Zapatistas of the EZLN initially wanted their uprising to coincide with the anniversary of 1492 but, for reasons of military unreadiness, put off their action until 1994. They were, however, behind an act of symbolic reparation: the overturning of the statue of the conquistador Diego de Mazariega in the centre of San Cristobal de las Casas, the capital of the Chiapas, in 1992 by a crowd of indigenous peoples that had come down from the mountains. Politics, culture and history were intimately interlinked in the clashes around the cinquecentennial. But that would hardly have surprised Walter Benjamin . . .

THESIS VIII

The tradition of the oppressed teaches us that the 'state of emergency' in which we live is not the exception but the rule. We must attain to a conception of history that accords with this insight. Then we will clearly see that it is our task to bring about a real state of emergency, and this will improve our position in the struggle against

> *Fascism. One reason Fascism has a chance is that, in the name of progress, its opponents treat it as a historical norm. The current amazement that the things we are experiencing are 'still' possible in the twentieth century is not philosophical. This amazement is not the beginning of knowledge – unless it is the knowledge that the view of history which gives rise to it is untenable.*

Benjamin is here contrasting two conceptions of history, with clear political implications for the present: on the one hand, the cosy 'progressive' doctrine, for which historical progress, the development of societies towards more democracy, freedom or peace is the norm, and, on the other, the one for which he himself argues, which takes as its standpoint the tradition of the oppressed for whom the norm or rule of history is the oppression, barbarism and violence of the victors.

The two conceptions react in diametrically opposing ways to Fascism. For the former, it is an exception to the norm of progress, an inexplicable 'regression', a parenthesis in the onward march of humanity. For the latter, it is the most recent and brutal expression of the 'permanent state of emergency' that is the history of class oppression. Benjamin was doubtless influenced by the ideas of Carl Schmitt in *Political Theology* (1921), a work which interested him greatly, particularly for its identification of sovereignty – whether it be monarchical, dictatorial or republican – with the state of emergency: he is sovereign who has executive power over the state of emergency. We find this theme also in *The Origin of German Tragic Drama*: after citing Carl Schmitt, Benjamin observes, writing of the Counter-Reformation, that 'the ruler is designated from the outset as the holder of dictatorial power if war, revolt or other catastrophes should lead to a state of emergency'. He adds a few pages later: 'The theory of sovereignty which takes as its example the special case in which dictatorial powers are unfolded, positively demands the completion of the image of the sovereign, as tyrant.' These observations from the 1920s were doubtless in Benjamin's mind when in 1940 he was pondering the nature of the Third Reich.[71]

Such a view of things makes it possible to situate Fascism as a further stage in the triumphal procession of the victors, as the head of the Medusa, as the supreme, final face of the recurrent barbarism of the powerful. Its great failing, however, is that it does not bring out the novelty of Fascism, particularly in its

Hitlerian variant, in relation to the old forms of domination: what the Frankfurt School was to call 'total administration' and Hannah Arendt 'totalitarianism'. We must say, in Benjamin's defence, that the most characteristic manifestations of this historical novelty – the concentration camp system, the death factories and the industrial extermination of Jews and Gypsies – would only develop in all their terrifying potency after his death, during the years 1941–45.

One of the trump cards of Fascism was, as Benjamin stressed, the incomprehension shown by its opponents, inspired as they were by the ideology of progress. He is thinking of the Left here, as is made explicit in one of the preparatory notes for the 'Theses'.[72] Two examples will allow us to illustrate what he is referring to.

For Social Democracy, Fascism was a vestige of the past; it was anachronistic and pre-modern. In his writings of the 1920s, Karl Kautsky explained that Fascism was possible only in a semi-agrarian country like Italy, but could never prevail in a modern, industrialized nation like Germany.

For its part, the official (Stalinist) Communist movement was convinced that Hitler's victory of 1933 was ephemeral: it was a matter of a few weeks or a few months before the Nazi regime would be swept away by the workers' movement and progressive forces under the leadership of the KPD (German Communist Party).

Benjamin had grasped perfectly the modernity of Fascism, its intimate relation with contemporary industrial-capitalist society. Hence his critique of those – the same people – who were astonished that Fascism should 'still' be possible in the twentieth century, blinded as they were by the illusion that scientific, industrial and technical progress was incompatible with social and political barbarism. This astonishment is not the *thaumazein* of Aristotle, the source of all philosophical knowledge: it leads only to a failure to understand Fascism, and hence it leads to defeat.

What is needed, observes Benjamin in one of the preparatory notes, is a theory of history on the basis of which Fascism can be examined (*gesichtet*).[73] Only a conception without progressivist illusions can account for a phenomenon like Fascism that is deeply rooted in modern industrial and technical 'progress' and was, ultimately, possible *only* in the twentieth century. The understanding that Fascism can triumph in the most 'civilized' countries and that 'progress' will not automatically cause it to disappear will enable us, he thinks, to improve our position in the anti-Fascist struggle – a struggle whose ultimate aim is to produce 'the *real* state of emergency' or, more literally, the real 'state of exception' [*Ausnahmezustand*], that is, the abolition of domination, the classless society.[74]

This utopian 'state of exception' is prefigured by all the revolts and uprisings that interrupt, if only for a brief moment, the triumphal procession of the powerful. It is also prefigured playfully – and even grotesquely – in certain popular celebrations, such as carnival. Benjamin is in accord here with Mikhail Bakhtin. In a story from the 1920s entitled *Gespräch über dem Corso*, he writes, 'The carnival is an exceptional state [*Ausnahmezustand*]. A descendant of the ancient saturnalia, when everything was turned upside down and the lords waited on the slaves. But an exceptional state really only stands out against an ordinary one.'[75]

Except, of course, for the fact that the carnavalesque interlude was merely a way of letting off steam, and the masters recovered their places 'on top' once the festival was over. Clearly, the aim of the '*real* state of exception', in which there would no longer be any 'top' or 'bottom', any masters or slaves, was quite different.

THESIS IX

Mein Flügel ist zum Schwung bereit
Ich kehrte gern zurück
Denn blieb' ich auch lebedige Zeit
Ich hätte wenig Glück

(My wing is ready for a flight,
I'm all for turning back;
For, even staying timeless time,
I'd have but little luck.)
                                        Gerhard Scholem,
                                'Greetings from the Angelus'

There is a picture by Klee called Angelus Novus. *It shows an angel who seems about to move away from something he stares at. His eyes are wide, his mouth is open, his wings are spread. This is how the angel of history must look. His face is*

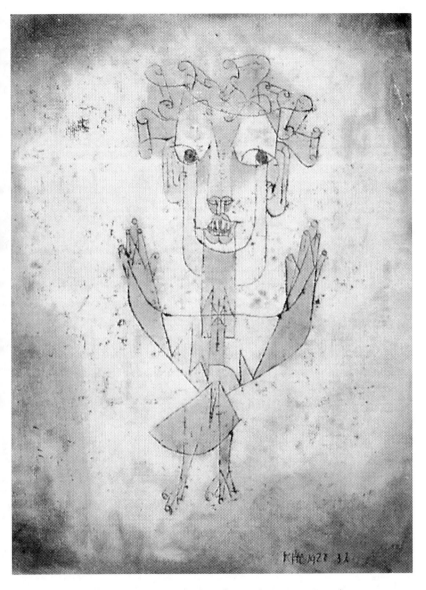

Paul Klee, *Angelus Novus*, 1920. The Israel Museum, Jerusalem.
© ADAGP, Paris 2001.

turned towards the past. Where a chain of events appears before us, he sees one single catastrophe, which keeps piling wreckage upon wreckage and hurls it at its feet. The angel would like to stay, awaken the dead, and make whole what has been smashed. But a storm is blowing from Paradise and has got caught in his wings; it is so strong that the angel can no longer close them. This storm drives him irresistibly into the future, to which his back is turned, while the pile of debris before him grows towards the sky. What we call progress is this storm.

This is Benjamin's best-known text and it has been quoted, interpreted and utilized on countless occasions and in the most diverse contexts. Quite clearly, it has seized the imagination of our age – doubtless because it touches upon something profound in the crisis of modern culture. But also because it has a prophetic dimension: its tragic warning seems to prefigure Auschwitz and Hiroshima, the two greatest catastrophes of human history, the two most monstrous ruins that crowned the pile 'grow[ing] towards the sky'

This thesis sums up, 'as though in a focal point', the whole of the document. It is an allegory in the sense that its elements have no signification outside the role intentionally assigned to them by the author. Benjamin had been fascinated by religious allegories, particularly those of the *Trauerspiel*, the German classical drama in which allegory is 'the *facies hippocratica* of history' that offers itself to the spectator's gaze 'as a petrified, primordial landscape'.[76] Thesis IX is exactly this, word for word.

The thesis presents itself as the commentary on a painting by Paul Klee which Benjamin had acquired in his youth. In reality, what it describes bears very little relation to the painting: what is involved here is, in the main, the projection of his own feelings and ideas on to the German artist's subtle and austere picture.

In the construction of this text, Benjamin probably took his inspiration from certain passages, certain poetic images, in the *Fleurs du mal*. For example, these lines from poem LXXI ('A Fantastical Engraving') seem to describe the vision of humanity's past the Benjaminian angel perceives:

> . . . a graveyard's empty plain,
> Where lie, with pallid sunshine overhead,
> From old and modern times, the storied dead.

But the relationship of Thesis IX to Baudelaire is more profound. The meaning structure of allegory is based on a correspondence, in the Baude-lairian sense, between the sacred and the profane, between theology and politics, which runs through each of the images. For one of the figures of the allegory, the two meanings are given to us by the text itself: the profane counterpart to the storm blowing from Paradise is Progress, which is responsible for an unremitting catastrophe and a pile of ruins rising up to the sky. But for the others we have to find their social and political meaning by reference to other writings of Benjamin's.

The storm blowing from Paradise doubtless evokes the Fall and expulsion from the Garden of Eden. It is in these terms that Adorno and Horkheimer interpreted it in a passage in *Dialectic of Enlightenment* which picks up on Benjamin's image and idea, though they do not acknowledge the quotation: 'The angel with the fiery sword who drove man out of paradise and onto the path of technical progress is the very symbol of that progress.'[77] What is the secular equivalent of this lost paradise, from which progress is distancing us more and more? Several clues suggest to us that, for Benjamin, it is primitive classless society. In the article on Bachofen (1935) mentioned in the Intro-duction, he writes, with regard to ancient matriarchal communities, of a profoundly democratic and egalitarian 'communistic society at the dawn of history'.[78] And in the essay, 'Paris, The Capital of the Nineteenth Century', he comes back to this idea: the experiences of the classless society of prehistory laid down in the collective unconscious 'engender, through interpenetration with what is new, . . . utopia'.[79]

At the opposite extreme from Paradise lies Hell. This is not mentioned in Thesis IX, but several of Benjamin's texts suggest a correspondence between modernity – or progress – and infernal damnation. For example, in this passage from the 1938 text 'Central Park', made up of fragments on Baudelaire, which has some obvious affinities with Thesis IX, he writes: 'The concept of progress must be grounded in the idea of catastrophe. That things are "status quo" *is* the catastrophe . . . Strindberg's idea: hell is not something that awaits us, but *this life here and now*.'[80] In what sense? For Benjamin, in *The Arcades Project*, the quintessence of Hell is the eternal repetition of the same, the most fearful paradigm of which is to be found not in Christian theology, but in Greek mythology: Sisyphus and Tantalus, condemned to the eternal return of the same punishment. In this context, Benjamin quotes a passage from Engels, comparing the worker's interminable torture – compelled, as he is, endlessly to repeat the same mechanical movement – with the infernal punishment of Sisyphus. But this is not just something that afflicts the worker: the whole of modern society, dominated by commodities, is subject to repetition, to the *Immergleich* (always the same), disguised as novelty and fashion: in the realm of commodities, 'Humanity figures . . . as damned.'[81]

The Angel of History would like to halt, to bind the wounds of the victims crushed beneath the pile of ruins, but the storm carries it on inexorably towards the repetition of the past: to new catastrophes, new hecatombs, ever vaster and more destructive. It is striking to contrast the tragic gaze of Benjamin's Angel of History with the perfectly Olympian gaze of History as described by Schiller in one of the canonical texts of the progressive *Aufklärung* which the author of the 'Theses' doubtless knew by heart, 'Was heisst und zu welchem Ende studiert man Universalgeschichte?' (1789):

> Like Homer's Zeus, she [History] gazes down with equal serenity on the bloody works of war and on peaceful people who innocently obtain their nourishment from the milk of their herds. However irregularly man's freedom appears to be governing the course of the world, she calmly observes the confused spectacle; for her far-reaching gaze detects already from afar how this erratically meandering freedom is being steered along the lines of necessity.[82]

One cannot but assume that Benjamin chose deliberately to take the opposite stance to this famous passage, opposing the despairing attitude of his Marxist/ Jewish angel to the serene and peaceful gaze of Schiller's Zeus.

The ruins at issue here are not, as they were for the Romantic painters or poets, an object of aesthetic contemplation, but a poignant image of the catastrophes, massacres and other bloody works of history. In choosing this term, Benjamin was probably pursuing an implicit confrontation with Hegel's philosophy of history, that immense rationalistic theodicy which legitimated every 'ruin' and every historical infamy as a necessary stage in the triumphal march of Reason, as an unavoidable moment of humanity's Progress towards the Consciousness of Freedom: *Weltgeschichte ist Weltgericht*

Odilon Redon, *The Fallen Angel*. Before 1880.
Musée des Beaux-Arts, Bordeaux.

('World history [is] the world's court of judgement').[83] According to Hegel,
history looks at first sight like an immense field of ruins, on which 'the untold
miseries of individual human beings' resound, an altar 'on which the
happiness of nations . . . and the virtue of individuals are slaughtered'. Given
this 'most terrifying picture', this 'distant spectacle of confusion and wreckage', one might tend towards 'an extreme pitch of hopeless sorrow with no
redeeming circumstances to counterbalance it', a deep-seated sense of revolt
and moral affliction. Yet, we must go beyond these first 'negative results' and
lift ourselves above these 'sentimental reflections' to grasp the essential point:
namely, that these ruins are merely means in the service of the 'substantial
destiny . . . the true result of world history', the realization of universal
Spirit.[84]

   Benjamin's approach consists precisely in standing this view of history on
its head, in demystifying progress and riveting a gaze imbued with a deep,

inconsolable sadness – but also with a profound moral revulsion – on the ruins it produces. These no longer bear witness, as in Hegel, to the 'transience of empires' – Hegel mentions the empires of Carthage, Palmyra, Persepolis and Rome[85] – but are, rather, an allusion to history's great massacres – hence the reference to 'the dead' – and to the cities destroyed by war: from Jerusalem, destroyed by the Romans, to the ruins of Guernica and Madrid, the towns and cities of Republican Spain bombed by the Luftwaffe in 1936–37.

Why refer to Progress as a 'storm'? The term also appears in Hegel, who describes 'the tumult of world events' as a 'storm blowing over the present'. But in Benjamin the word is probably borrowed from biblical language, where it evokes catastrophe and destruction: it was by a storm that humanity was drowned in the Flood and by a firestorm that Sodom and Gomorrah were swept away. The comparison between the Flood and Nazism is, moreover, suggested by Benjamin in a letter of January 1937 to Scholem, in which he compares his book *Deutsche Menschen* to an 'ark' built 'after the Jewish fashion' – in the face of 'the rising Fascist flood'.[86]

But this term also evokes the fact that, for conformist ideology, Progress is a 'natural, phenomenon, governed by the laws of nature, and as such inevitable and irresistible'. In one of the preparatory notes for the 'Theses', Benjamin explicitly criticizes this positivistic, 'naturalistic' approach of historical evolutionism: 'The project of discovering "laws" for the course of historical events is not the only means – and hardly the most subtle – of assimilating historiography to natural science.'[87]

How is this storm to be halted, how is Progress to be interrupted in its unstoppable forward march? As ever, Benjamin's answer is twofold: religious and secular. In the theological sphere, this is a task for the Messiah; its secular equivalent or *correspondant* is none other than *Revolution*. The messianic/revolutionary interruption of Progress is, then, Benjamin's response to the threats to the human race posed by the continuance of the evil storm, the imminence of new catastrophes. We are in 1940, a few months away from the beginning of the Final Solution. A non-religious image, in Benjamin's preparatory notes, sums up this idea and, in doing so, runs counter to the commonplace assumptions of the 'progressive' Left: 'Marx says that revolutions are the locomotive of world history. But perhaps it is quite otherwise. Perhaps revolutions are an attempt by the passengers on this train – namely, the human race – to activate the emergency brake.'[88] The image suggests implicitly that if humanity were to allow the train to follow its course – already mapped out by the steel structure of the rails – and if nothing halted its headlong dash, we would be heading straight for disaster, for a crash or a plunge into the abyss.

What the Angel of History is impotent to achieve only the Messiah will be able to accomplish: to still the storm, to bandage the wounded, reawaken the dead and mend what has been put asunder (*das Zeschlagene zusammenfügen*). In Scholem's view, this formulation contains an implicit reference to the cabbalistic doctrine of *tikkun,* the Messianic restitution of the original state of divine harmony broken by the *shevirat ha kelim,* the 'breaking of the vessels' – a doctrine Benjamin knew from the article 'Kabbalah' published by his friend in 1932 in the *Encyclopaedia Judaica* (in German).[89]

And what is the political counterpart (*correspondant*) to this mystical restitution, to this restoration of the lost paradise, to this messianic kingdom? The answer is given in the preparatory notes: 'A genuinely messianic face must be restored to the concept of classless society and, to be sure, in the interest of furthering the revolutionary politics of the proletariat itself'; because it is only by realizing its messianic significance that one can avoid the pitfalls of 'progressive' ideology.[90]

This communist society of the future is, to a certain degree, the return to primitive communism, to the first form of classless society 'at the dawn of history'. Scholem is therefore right in saying that, for Benjamin, 'Paradise is at once the origin and primal past (*Urvergangenheit*) of humanity as well as the utopian image of the future of his redemption', but it seems to me that he is wrong to add that we have here a conception of the historical process that is 'cyclical rather than dialectical'. For Benjamin, the classless society of the future – the new Paradise – is not the return pure and simple to the society of prehistory: it contains in itself, as dialectical synthesis, the whole of humanity's past. True universal history, based on the universal remembrance of all victims without exception – the secular equivalent of the resurrection of the dead – will be possible only in the future classless society.[91]

The connection made here between the messianic era and the future classless society – like the connection between the other 'correspondences' in the 1940 'Theses' – cannot be understood solely in terms of secularization.

There is, in Benjamin, a relation of reciprocal reversibility, of mutual translation between the religious and the political that cannot be unilaterally reduced: in a system of communicating vessels, the fluid is necessarily present in all the arms simultaneously.

THESIS X

The themes which monastic discipline assigned to friars for meditation were designed to turn them away from the world and its affairs. The thoughts we are developing here have a similar aim. At a moment when the politicians in whom the opponents of Fascism had placed their hopes are prostrate, and confirm their defeat by betraying their own cause, these observations are intended to extricate the political worldlings from the snares in which the traitors have entangled them. The assumption here is that those politicians' stubborn faith in progress, their confidence in their 'base in the masses', and, finally, their servile integration in an uncontrollable apparatus are three aspects of the same thing. This consideration is meant to suggest the high price our customary mode of thought will have to pay for a conception of history that avoids any complicity with the concept of history to which those politicians still adhere.

In this thesis Benjamin resumes his polemic with the dominant conceptions within the Left, referring implicitly to the traumatic event that was doubtless the immediate motivation for the drafting of the document: the Molotov–Ribbentrop pact.

The first sentence is rather paradoxical: are readers of the 'Theses' also to be turned away from the world like monks? Is action to be abandoned in favour of 'meditation'? Such an interpretation would be in total contradiction with the other theses. In our view, another reading seems possible. The method of the theses could be said to consist in (a) stepping back, distancing oneself and acquiring perspective on current political events, not in order to ignore them, but to find their deep causes, and (b) turning away from the illusions and 'temptations' of the century, the cosy, seductive doctrines of progress. Benjamin seems inspired by ascetic exigencies and appears to betray a certain intransigence where 'worldly' compromises are concerned. But the analogy he chooses here is indeed a strange one and is susceptible of much misunderstanding.

The expression 'the politicians in whom the opponents of Fascism had placed their hopes' is quite clear: he is referring to the (Stalinist) Communists, who have 'betray[ed] their own cause' by making a pact with Hitler. More precisely, the sentence refers to the KPD (German Communist Party), which, unlike the Soviet Communist Party, was 'prostrate'. The hope for a coherent fight against Fascism lay, in Benjamin's view, much more with the Communist movement, than with Social Democracy. Now, the pact had sounded the death knell of that hope. The 'betrayal' here refers not just to the agreement between Molotov and Ribbentrop, but also to its legitimation by the Communist Parties, who were to adopt the Soviet 'line'.[92] It does not in any way for Benjamin mean the break with Communism or Marxism, as Somma Morgenstern believes he understood – but the definitive and irrevocable dissociation of Soviet reality from the Communist idea.[93] In fact, Benjamin shares his categorical condemnation of the pact with several other dissident German Communists exiled in Paris, such as his friend Heinrich Blücher (husband of Hannah Arendt), Willy Münzenberg and Manes Sperber.[94]

It is the aim of the 'Theses' to free *das politische Weltkind* from the traps into which he has fallen. This somewhat odd expression, which originates in a poem by Goethe and which is pluralized here in Harry Zohn's translation as 'the political worldlings', is difficult to translate. Among Benjamin's French translators, Maurice de Gandillac renders it literally as '*l'enfant politique du monde*', while Pierre Missac rather arbitrarily proposes '*les braves citoyens*'. However, Benjamin's own French translation gives us the precise sense of his meaning. He renders the expression as '*les enfants du siècle*', that is to say the twentieth-century generation – his own.

Benjamin sets out to free that generation from the snares [*aus den Netzen*] in which the politicians (his French translation, '*la gauche*', is more explicit, referring as it does to the great workers' parties) have entangled it. We again meet an image from Nietzsche's *Untimely Observations* here, according to which the critical historian – the one who dares to swim against the tide – must break with the 'lies' which, 'all around him, . . . spin their glittering nets'.[95] In his French translation, Benjamin does not speak of 'snares' or 'nets', but substitutes the word '*promesses*': the illusory promises of the Left have had a paralysing effect; they neutralize people's efforts and prevent them from acting.

These illusions manifest themselves in three forms, which all derive from the same conception of history: blind faith in progress, the belief in the support of the masses as something ensured in advance, and submission to an uncontrollable apparatus – Benjamin translates this as '*confiance aveugle dans le parti*' (blind trust in the party). He touches here on a crucial question: bureaucracy – the uncontrollable bureaucratic machine that runs the workers' parties – and the fetishism of the party, which has become an end in itself and is supposed infallible, particularly in the Stalinized Communist movement.

In one of the preparatory notes, Benjamin writes of 'trust in quantitative accumulation' which 'underlies both the obstinate faith in progress and trust in the 'base in the masses [*Massenbasis*]'.[96] Benjamin is here criticizing the essential article of faith of unimaginative, reductionist Marxism common to the two main strands of the Left: the quantitative accumulation of productive forces, of the gains of the labour movement, of the number of party members and voters in a movement of linear, irresistible, 'automatic' progress. When seen that way, historical materialism is reduced to the puppet/automaton described in Thesis I.

The conclusion to the thesis is a denunciation of the politicians who persist in – who cling to – this tragically illusory view of history. In his translation, Benjamin describes them as '*ceux qui . . . n'ont rien appris*':[97] those who have learned nothing, that is to say, those who have resisted drawing any lessons from their terrible defeat at the hands of Nazism.

Benjamin refers in this thesis to the Left in general and, implicitly, to the Communist Parties. In other theses, the target of his criticism is Social Democracy. To what extent did he know or take his inspiration from dissident currents on the Left? We have seen that, in the 1930s, he often showed an interest in the writings of Trotsky, and Karl Korsch was one of his main Marxist references in *The Arcades Project* – not to mention some of his friends, such as Heinrich Blücher, who were close to the German Communist opposition led by Heinrich Brandler.

We may note some instances when Benjamin's critiques – for example, of the betrayal constituted by the 1939 Pact or of the blind submission to the party's bureaucratic apparatus – converge with those of these Communist dissidents. But the 'Theses' call into question the ideology of progress in a much deeper and more thoroughgoing way than the critical ideas advanced by most of these dissident Marxist tendencies.

From this point of view, the position Benjamin occupies in the field of Marxism in 1939–40 is unique, unprecedented and unmatched. He is isolated, being too far ahead of his time. It will be several decades before his concerns being to find an echo, in the 1960s, among rebellious youth and Left-wing intellectuals. The only exception are his friends in the Frankfurt School, particularly in their writings in the period 1941–48, but they are far from sharing his commitment to the class struggle. If *Dialectic of Enlightenment* – and also Adorno's *Minima Moralia* – owe much to Benjamin, the text that comes closest to the 'Theses "On the Concept of History"' – even if it does not refer to the same theological and messianic sources – is Horkheimer's 'Authoritarian State', published in the Institute of Social Research's 1942 homage to Benjamin. It is, by its explicit political radicalism, a relatively 'atypical' document. According to Horkheimer, since 'the revolutionary conditions have always been ripe', the imperative of putting an end to the horror 'was always appropriate'. The radical transformation of society, the end of exploitation, 'are not a further acceleration of progress, but a qualitive leap out of the dimension of progress'.[98]

THESIS XI

The conformism which has marked the Social Democrats from the beginning attaches not only to their political tactics but to their economic views as well. It is one reason for the eventual breakdown of their party. Nothing has so corrupted the German working class as the notion that it was moving with the current. It regarded technological development as the driving force of the stream with which it thought it was moving. From there it was but a step to the illusion that the factory work ostensibly furthering technological progress constituted a political achievement. The old Protestant work ethic was resurrected among German workers in secularized form. The Gotha Programme already bears traces of this confusion, defining labour as 'the source of all wealth and all culture'. Smelling a rat, Marx countered that 'the man who possesses no other property than his labour power' must of necessity become 'the slave of other men who have made themselves owners'. Yet the confusion spread, and soon thereafter Josef Dietzgen proclaimed: 'The saviour of modern times is called work. The . . . perfecting . . . of the labour process constitutes the wealth which can now do what no redeemer has ever been able to accomplish.' This vulgar-Marxist conception of the nature of labour scarcely considers the question of how its products could ever benefit the workers when they are beyond the means of those workers. It recognizes only the progress in mastering nature, not the retrogression of society; it already displays the technocratic features that later emerge in Fascism. Among these is a conception of nature which differs ominously from the one advocated by socialist utopias prior to the Revolution of 1848. The new conception of labour is tantamount to the exploitation of nature, which, with naïve complacency, is contrasted with the exploitation of the proletariat. Compared to this positivistic view, Fourier's fantasies, which have so often been ridiculed, prove surprisingly sound. According to Fourier, cooperative labour would increase efficiency to such an extent that four moons would illuminate the sky at night, the polar ice caps would recede, seawater would no longer taste salty, and beasts of prey would do man's bidding. All this illustrates a kind of labour which, far from exploiting nature, would help her give birth to the creations that now lie dormant in her womb. The sort of nature that (as Dietzgen puts it) 'exists gratis', is a complement to the corrupted conception of labour.

If, in Thesis X, Benjamin is largely taking issue with Stalinist conformism, in Thesis XI he rounds on the conformism of the Social Democrats. In each case his starting point is the will to understand the deep causes of the defeat of the German labour movement at the hands of Hitlerian Fascism.

The ideology of 'work' promoted by Social Democracy was merely a secularized form of the Protestant work ethic, whose close connections – by *elective affinity* – to the spirit of capitalism had been laid bare by the researches of Max Weber, which Benjamin knew well. This acritical celebration of 'labour as "the source of all wealth . . ." ' disregards the fact that, in the capitalist system, the worker is reduced to a condition of modern slavery and finds himself divested, by the propertied classes, of the wealth he produces. Benjamin draws on both Weber and Marx to criticize the conformist posture of Social Democracy in relation to industrial-capitalist production.

The cult of work and industry is, at the same time, a cult of technical progress – a theme with which Benjamin had been intensely concerned since the 1920s. In the essay on Fuchs of 1937, a text that already contains the main themes of Thesis XI, he stresses the contrast between the 'questionable . . . optimism' of Social Democracy, which ignores the destructive energy of technology – particularly 'the technology of war'[99] – and the 'vision . . . which flashed on the consciousness' of Marx and Engels of the potential evolution of capitalism towards barbarism.[100]

Benjamin writes in Thesis XI of the positivism of the Social Democratic ideology of progress. The essay on Fuchs had already made reference to the positivism, Darwinism and evolutionism of European Social Democracy and he referred there to the Italian Enrico Ferri (who saw the party's tactics as conforming to the laws of nature) as a typical example.

A few passages from Ferri's work will illustrate the kind of language Benjamin was taking issue with. According to the Italian social positivist thinker, 'What scientific socialism can affirm, and what it does affirm, with mathematical certainty, is that the current, the trajectory of human evolution is in a general sense indicated and foreseen by socialism, that is to say, in the sense of a continuous, progressive preponderance of the interests and benefit of the species over those of the individual . . .' Socialism 'is a natural and spontaneous product of human evolution which is already in the process of formation, general lines of which are already drawn . . .'[101] One does, in fact, find very similar formulations in the writings of Kautsky and Plekhanov, and also of Engels, whom Benjamin does not mention.[102] Thesis XI, like the essay on Fuchs, attacks this type of deterministic, evolutionist doctrine that leads to the idea that the victory of the party is assured from the outset. Similarly, in a variant, Benjamin quotes a passage from Dietzgen, '*Wir warten unsere Zeit ab*' [We are biding our time].[103]

The polemic of Thesis XI is directed, then, against the illusion of swimming with the tide of technical development – a tide that is supposed to lead necessarily to the triumph of 'scientific' socialism (in the positivist sense of the term). This optimistic fatalism could lead the labour movement only to passivity and *attentisme*, when the need was, rather, to intervene urgently, to act rapidly before it was too late, before the looming catastrophe arrived. This was one of the reasons for the debacle of 1933.

This evolutionary-positivist conception of history 'recognizes only the progress in the domination of nature, not social regression'. We find it again later in another form in the technocratic ideology of Fascism. Unlike so many other Marxists, Benjamin had clearly perceived the modern, technically 'advanced' aspect of Nazism, combining the greatest technological 'progress' – particularly in the military field – with the most terrible social regressions. What was merely suggested in Thesis VIII is here explicitly affirmed: Fascism, in spite of its 'archaic' cultural manifestations, is a pathological manifestation of industrial-capitalist modernity, basing itself on the great technical achievements of the twentieth century,[104] though this does not mean, of course, that modernity for Benjamin cannot take other forms, or that technical progress is necessarily harmful.

In his famous – and, in many ways, remarkable – critical essay on Benjamin, Jürgen Habermas wrote: 'Historical materialism, which reckons on progressive steps not only in the dimension of productive forces but in that of domination as well, cannot be covered over with an anti-evolutionary conception of history as with a monk's cowl.'[105] This assertion seems debatable in my view. It raises many questions, such as, for example:

1. Is it certain we can speak of 'progress' in the field of forms of domination – *Herrschaft* – if we compare the twentieth century – the era of totalitarianisms and genocides – with the nineteenth?

2. Is historical materialism necessarily an evolutionary doctrine? In Marx's own writings, do we not find both evolutionary and non-evolutionary texts – such as his last writings on Russia, for example? And if it is true that the evolutionary – and positivist – tendencies have predominated in Marxism since the end of the nineteenth century, do we not also find eminent representatives of a non-evolutionary historical materialism, from Antonio Labriola and Rosa Luxemburg to the Frankfurt School itself to which Habermas claims to be heir?

3. Is the critique of historical evolutionism and its faith in the irresistible progress of forms of domination necessarily an obscurantist regression into the past – a 'monk's cowl' – or is it, rather, in the light of the catastrophes of the twentieth century, a lucid vision of the dangers contained within modern civilization?

4. Is what is at stake in the emancipatory struggles for historical materialism an improvement or 'progress' in the forms of domination or, rather, the abolition of all *Herrschaft* of one human being over another, of one class over another – what Benjamin describes as the 'real state of emergency'? Unlike Max Weber, for Benjamin the concept of *Herrschaft* does not refer to the abstract possibility of making oneself obeyed,[106] but is something more concrete and radical (as it is, for example, in Machiavelli): the authoritarian exercise of power by an – in each case specific – combination of manipulation and violence. And, indeed, he often uses the more explicit term, *Unterdrückung*, meaning 'oppression'. In the 'Theses' and the preparatory notes known as the 'Paralipomena', the ruling classes are referred to at times as *die Herrschenden*, the dominant, and at others as *die Unterdrücker*, the oppressors. The Frankfurt School's critique of domination was no doubt influenced by Benjamin, but Adorno and Horkheimer stress not so much class power – the combination of domination and exploitation – as statist authoritarianism, 'total administration'. However, all share the Marxian preoccupation with the domination exerted by alienated impersonal structures, such as capital or the commodity.

The last part of Thesis XI is extraordinarily topical: it involves a radical critique of the capitalist exploitation of nature and the glorification of that exploitation by vulgar Marxism, which is positivist and technocratic in inspiration. In this field, too, Benjamin occupies a unique place in the panorama of Marxist thinking in the first half of the century. Anticipating the ecological preoccupations of the late twentieth century, he dreams of a new pact between humans and their environment.

Benjamin opposes the 'progressive' ideology of a certain 'scientific' socialism – represented here by the German social positivist Joseph Dietzgen, long forgotten today, but immensely popular in German Social Democracy at the turn of the century (and often quoted by Lenin in *Materialism and Empirio-Criticism*, his most 'orthodox' work) – which reduces nature to an industrial raw material, to a commodity that 'exists gratis', an object for unlimited domination and exploitation. Against this approach, Benjamin does not hesitate to appeal to the utopias of the first socialists – *Vormärz*, before the Revolution of March 1848 – and, in particular, the fantastical dreams of Fourier (to which André Breton will pay enthusiastic tribute some ten years later). Benjamin, who is sensitive to the poetry and enchantment of these dreams, interprets them as the intuiting of a different – non-destructive – relation to nature, leading both to new scientific discoveries – electricity might be an example of the virtual energy 'that now lie[s] dormant in . . . [nature's] bosom' – and to the re-establishment of the lost harmony between society and the natural environment.

Benjamin's interest in, and admiration for, Fourier grew steadily throughout the 1930s. *The Arcades Project* casts light on the points made in Thesis XI: Benjamin does not counterpoise Fourier to Marx – he carefully records all the instances when Marx or Engels praise the 'colossal conception of man' of the inventor of the phalansteries and his brilliant 'intuitions of a new world' – but to the vulgar Marxism shared by the main currents of the Left.[107] Linking the abolition of the exploitation of human labour closely with that of the exploitation of nature, Benjamin saw the ' "impassioned work" of the Harmonians', inspired by 'children's play', as the utopian model for emancipated activity. 'To have instituted play as the canon of a labour no longer rooted in exploitation,' he wrote, 'is one of the great merits of Fourier. Such work inspired by play aims not at the propagation of values, but at the amelioration of nature . . . An earth that was cultivated according to such an image would cease to be part of "a world where action is never the sister of the dream." '[108]

In *The Arcades Project* the name of Fourier is associated with that of Bachofen, who had discovered the ancestral image of this reconciliation in matriarchal society in the form of the cult of nature as bountiful mother – in radical opposition to the lethal (*mörderisch*) conception of the exploitation of nature, dominant since the nineteenth century. In the ideal harmony between society and nature the utopian socialist dreamt of, Benjamin perceives reminiscences of a lost prehistoric paradise. This is why, in the essay, 'Paris, the Capital of the Nineteenth Century' (1939), he refers to Fourier as an example of the meeting of the old and the new in a utopia that breathes new life into the primeval (*uralt*) symbols of desire.[109]

SYSTÈME DE FOURIER.

Fourier's System,
an engraving published in J. Grandville, *Un autre monde* (Paris, 1844).

Thesis XII

We need history, but our need for it differs from that of the jaded idlers in the garden of knowledge.
        Nietzsche, *On the Advantages and Disadvantages of History for Life*

The subject of historical knowledge is the struggling, oppressed class itself. Marx presents it as the last enslaved class – the avenger that completes the task of liberation in the name of generations of the downtrodden. This conviction, which had a brief resurgence in the Spartacus League, has always been objectionable to Social Democrats. Within three decades they managed to erase the name of Blanqui almost entirely, though at the sound of that name the preceding century had quaked. The Social Democrats preferred to cast the working class in the role of a redeemer of future generations, in this way cutting the sinews of its greatest strength. This indoctrination made the working class forget both its hatred and its spirit of sacrifice, for both are nourished by the image of enslaved ancestors rather than by the ideal of liberated grandchildren.

The epigraph is from the Nietzsche text we have mentioned several times already. The quotation contains only the critical part, but it is interesting to consider the alternative he offers in the rest of his 1873 essay. According to Nietzsche, history – in the sense of historiography – must not be a luxury, a casual stroll or a matter of archaeological curiosity, but must be of use in the present: 'We need history for life and action . . .' He describes his considerations on history as 'untimely', because they 'act against the age and so have an effect on the age to the advantage, it is to be hoped, of a coming age'.[110] These remarks match Benjamin's intentions perfectly.

The first sentence here, on the subject of knowledge, is reminiscent of an idea that runs through the principal writings of Rosa Luxemburg: class consciousness – and, therefore, knowledge – is the product, above all, of the practice of struggle, of the active experience of the working class. This is clearly distinct from the proposition, common to Karl Kautsky and to Lenin in *What Is to Be Done?* (1902), that regards knowledge – or socialist consciousness – as something which has to be introduced into the class 'from outside' by intellectuals and theorists. There is nothing to suggest that

Benjamin read the writings of Rosa Luxemburg – he does not quote them anywhere – but he doubtless learned of her ideas from the presentation Georg Lukács made of them in several chapters of *History and Class Consciousness* (1923).

It is in this same work – whose importance in Benjamin's 'conversion' to Marxism we are already aware of – that we find a second possible meaning of Thesis XII: I have in mind Lukács's polemic against the conception of historical materialism as 'neutral' scientific knowledge proposed by the theorists of Social Democracy, Karl Kautsky and Rudolf Hilferding. According to *History and Class Consciousness*, Marxism represents a higher form of knowledge because it adopts the class standpoint of the proletariat, which is both the subject of historical action and the subject of knowledge. Benjamin's text repeats passages from Lukács almost verbatim, and we might wonder whether when he writes 'Marx' in Thesis XII, we should not perhaps read 'Lukács'.[11]

The last class to struggle against oppression, and the class charged, according to Marx, with the 'task of liberation' – the proletariat – cannot, in Benjamin's view, fulfil that role if it forgets its martyred ancestors: there can be no struggle for the future without a memory of the past. This is the theme of the redemption of the victims of history which we have already met in Theses II, III and IV, in its dual theological and political sense.

Benjamin's stress on defeated ancestors may seem surprising. It is doubtless too unilateral, insofar as the struggle against oppression takes its inspiration equally from the victims of the past and from hopes for the generations to come – and also, if not predominantly, from solidarity with present generations. It puts one in mind of the Jewish imperative: *Zakhor*, remember! Remember your ancestors who were slaves in Egypt, massacred by Amalek, exiled to Babylon, enslaved by Titus, burned alive by the Crusaders and murdered in the pogroms. We encounter this cult of martyrs, in another form, in Christianity, which made a crucified prophet its Messiah and his tortured disciples its saints. But the workers' movement itself has followed this paradigm in entirely secular form. Faithfulness to the memory of the 'Chicago martyrs' – the syndicalists and anarchists executed, in a parody of justice, by the American authorities in 1887 – inspired the ritual of May Day throughout the twentieth century. And we know how important the memory of the

עֲבָדִים הָיִינוּ לְפַרְעֹה בְּמִצְרָיִם · וַיּוֹצִיאֵנוּ יְ
אֱלֹהֵינוּ מִשָּׁם בְּיָד חֲזָקָה וּבִזְרוֹעַ
נְטוּיָה · וְאִלוּ לֹא הוֹצִיא הַקָּדוֹשׁ בָּרוּךְ הוּא אֶת

The Jewish slaves in Egypt. Seventeenth-century Haggadah.

murders of Karl Liebknecht and Rosa Luxemburg in 1919 was for the Communist movement in its early years. But it is perhaps Latin America that provides the most impressive example of the inspirational role of past victims, if one thinks of the place such figures as José Marti, Emiliano Zapata, Augusto Sandino, Farabundo Marti and, more recently, Ernesto Che Guevara have assumed in the revolutionary imagination of the last thirty years. If we think of all these examples, and many others we might cite, Benjamin's assertion that struggles are inspired more by the living, concrete memory of enslaved ancestors than by the – as yet abstract – thought of generations to come, appears less paradoxical.

The collective memory of the defeated differs from the various state pantheons to the glory of national heroes not just by the nature of the figures concerned or their message and their position in the field of social conflict, but also by the fact that it has, in Benjamin's view, a subversive significance only insofar as it is not exploited in the service of any form of power.

It is clear the remembrance of victims is not, for him, either a melancholic jeremiad or a mystical meditation. It has meaning only if it becomes a source of moral and spiritual energy for those in struggle today. This is the dialectic between past and present already suggested by Thesis IV, and it is of significance, particularly, for the fight against Fascism which draws its strength from the tradition of the oppressed. During a conversation with Brecht on the crimes of the Nazis in 1938, Benjamin notes: 'While he was speaking like this I felt a power being exercised over me which was equal in strength to the power of fascism, a power that sprang from depths of history no less deep than the power of the fascists.'[112]

To avoid misunderstandings, it may be helpful to go back to the terms 'hatred' and 'vengeance' used by Benjamin. We may wonder whether he is not, in using these terms, responding implicitly to Nietzsche. As we know, Nietzsche applied the term *ressentiment* to the 'thirst for vengeance and hatred' of the oppressed, the downtrodden and the enslaved. From his aristocratic point of view, theirs was a 'slave revolt in morals', based on envy, rancour and impotence, which had its origin among the Jews, that 'priestly people of *ressentiment par excellence*'.[113] For Benjamin the emotions of the oppressed, far from being the expression of an envious *ressentiment* or an impotent rancour, are a source of action, of active revolt, of revolutionary praxis. The concept of 'hatred' refers above all to indignation at past and present suffering, and to unyielding hostility to oppression – particularly in its latest and most terrifying manifestation: Fascism. One cannot struggle against the Third Reich, Benjamin seems to be saying, without a profound aversion for Nazism whose roots are sunk in past struggles. Like Marx in *Capital*, Benjamin is not preaching hatred of individuals, but of a system. As for avenging past victims, this can only mean the reparation of the wrong they suffered and the moral condemnation of those who inflicted it. The *Oxford English Dictionary* defines 'vengeance' as the 'retributive infliction of injury or punishment'. When we are speaking of an offence committed centuries or millennia ago, only moral punishment can be inflicted. Benjamin would not dream of avenging Spartacus and his comrades by punishing the Italian citizens of the twentieth century! On the other hand, the overthrow of Fascism – which presented itself as the heir to the Roman Empire – would *also* be a 'vengeance of history' for the crucified slaves and a challenge to the victory of the Roman patricians.

The important point for the author of the 'Theses' is that the last enslaved class, the proletariat, should perceive itself as heir to several centuries or millennia of struggle, to the lost battles of the slaves, serfs, peasants and artisans. The accumulated force of these endeavours becomes the explosive material with which the present emancipatory class will be able to interrupt the continuity of oppression.

Thesis XII appeals to two great historical witnesses to support its argument. The first is Spartacus or, rather, the Spartacus League (*Spartakusbund*), founded by Rosa Luxemburg and Karl Liebknecht, which in January 1919 assumed the leadership of a spontaneous workers' uprising in Berlin that was bloodily crushed by Gustav Noske, the Social Democratic interior minister. The aspect Benjamin stresses is the historical consciousness manifested in the name of the organization: the modern proletariat as heir to the slaves who rebelled against the Roman Empire. In this way the 1919 revolt becomes a moment in a universal battle that has lasted for thousands of years and not, as often depicted, a mere manifestation of post-war German domestic politics.

The other figure is Auguste Blanqui, 'at the sound of whose name the preceding century had quaked'. As a character, Blanqui, that *grand vaincu*, locked away in the prison cells of monarchies, republics and empires for decades, without ceasing to embody the staunchest revolutionary opposition to the existing order, fascinated Benjamin. The German text speaks not just of the 'sound' of his name, but of its *Erzklang*, its sounding out like brass, and this is doubtless a reference to the tocsin, the alarm bell this armed prophet figuratively sounded to warn the oppressed of imminent catastrophe.

Benjamin is interested not just in the historical figure, but also in the thinker, whose ideas were familiar to him from the splendid biography by Gustave Geoffroy. In defining the proletarians as 'modern slaves', Blanqui reveals a conception of history similar to that of the Spartakists. And he was, indeed, a staunch adversary of positivism and the ideologies of progress. In his book Geoffroy quotes some remarks by Blanqui from 1862: 'I am not one of those who claim that progress can be taken for granted, that humanity cannot

Auguste Blanqui. Painting by Mme Blanqui (1835).

go backwards . . . No, there is no inevitability; otherwise, the history of humanity, which is written hour by hour, would be entirely written in advance.'[114] It was perhaps with remarks of this kind in mind that Benjamin emphasized, in a passage in 'Central Park', that: 'the activities of a professional conspirator like Blanqui certainly do not presuppose any belief in progress – they merely presuppose a determination to do away with present injustice. This firm resolve to snatch humanity at the last moment from the catastrophe looming at every turn is characteristic of Blanqui . . .'[115]

In the French translation Benjamin himself made of the 'Theses' there is a last sentence that is absent from the German text; 'Our generation has learnt this to its cost, since the only image it is going to leave behind is that of a defeated generation. That will be its legacy to those who come after.'[116] This shows, explicitly and directly, that when he speaks of the defeated of history he is thinking also of himself and his generation. This casts light on the *Stimmung*, the mood, of the theses as a whole, as is suggested in one of his last letters, addressed to his friend S. Lackner on 5 May 1940: 'I've just finished a little essay on the concept of history, a work inspired not just by the new war, but by the whole experience of my generation, which must be one of the most sorely tried in history.'[117] In the same spirit, in one of the preparatory notes, he mentions Brecht's famous poem 'An die Nachgeborenen' ('To Those Born Later'), in which the writer calls on coming generations to remember the sufferings of his own. Benjamin adds this poignant commentary: 'We ask of those who will come after us not gratitude for our victories, but the remembrance of our defeats. This is a consolation – the only consolation afforded to those who no longer have any hope of being consoled.'[118]

Thesis XIII

Every day our cause becomes clearer and people get smarter.
                    Josef Dietzgen, *Social Democratic Philosophy*

Social Democratic theory and to an even greater extent its practice were shaped by a conception of progress which bore little relation to reality but made dogmatic claims.

Progress as pictured in the minds of the Social Democrats was, first of all, progress of humankind itself (and not just advances in human ability and knowledge). Second, it was something boundless (in keeping with an infinite perfectibility of humanity). Third, it was considered inevitable – something that automatically pursued a straight or spiral course. Each of these assumptions is controversial and open to criticism. But when the chips are down, criticism must penetrate beyond these assumptions and focus on what they have in common. The concept of mankind's historical progress cannot be sundered from the concept of its progression through a homogeneous, empty time. A critique of the concept of such a progression must underlie any criticism on the concept of progress itself.

The epigraph from Dietzgen – chosen once again as an ideal-typical example of limited, unimaginative Social Democratic 'progressism' – provides an illustration of an optimistic, linear view of history, fuelled by a superficial reading of the *Aufklärung*: the irresistible, uninterrupted ascent of 'enlightenment' and 'intelligence'. The tragic reality of Fascism gives the lie to this type of populistically tinged self-mystification.

Let us develop the three critiques, which the thesis does not expand upon, but which are based on an alternative view of history:

1. We must distinguish between the progress of knowledge and of capabilities (*Fähigkeiten*) and the progress of humanity itself: this latter involves a moral, social and political dimension that is not reducible to scientific, technical progress. The movement of history is necessarily heterogeneous – in *The History of the Russian Revolution*, a book Benjamin knew well, Trotsky would say its development was uneven and combined – and advances in one dimension of civilization may be accompanied by regressions in another (as Thesis XI had already noted).

2. If one wishes for the 'progress of humankind itself', one cannot trust to a process of gradual, infinite improvement, but must struggle for a radical break: the end of the age-old history of oppression or, in Marxian language, the end of prehistory. We should add that Benjamin does not use the expression 'end of prehistory' himself, but here refers – somewhat elliptically it must be said – to the possible coming of the 'real state of emergency' or, more precisely, state of exception [*Ausnahmezustand*]. Framing the issue in this way avoids evolutionism and teleology insofar as what is at issue here is an aim

being struggled for and an objective possibility, not the inevitable outcome of the 'laws of history'. And, indeed, as Benjamin writes in one of the most striking formulations in *The Arcades Project*: 'What our generation has learned: that capitalism will not die a natural death.'[119]

3. There is, therefore, no 'automatic' or 'continuous' progress: the only continuity is that of domination, and the automatism of history merely reproduces this ('the rule'). The only moments of freedom are interruptions, discontinuities, when the oppressed rise up and attempt to free themselves.[120]

To be effective, this critique of progressive doctrines has to attack their common foundation, their deepest root, their hidden quintessence: the dogma of an homogeneous empty temporality. In the following theses we shall see what this concept means and the alternative Benjamin proposes: namely, qualitative, heterogeneous, full time.

The stakes in this debate are far from purely theoretical and philosophical: at issue, stresses Benjamin, is a certain practical attitude that combines the optimism of progress with an absence of initiative, passivity and *attentisme*. An attitude which, as we have seen in connection with Thesis XI, finds its tragic dénouement in the German Left's capitulation without a fight to Hitler in 1933 or – to give an example Benjamin does not mention, but which was nonetheless in his mind at the point when he was drafting the 'Theses' – of (most of) the French Left's capitulation to Pétain in 1940.

Thesis XIV

Origin is the goal.
Karl Kraus, *Words in Verse*

History is the subject of a construction whose site is not homogeneous, empty time, but time filled full by now-time [Jetztzeit]. Thus, to Robespierre ancient Rome was a past charged with now-time, a past which he blasted out of the continuum of history. The French Revolution viewed itself as Rome reincarnate. It cited ancient Rome exactly the way fashion cites a bygone mode of dress. Fashion has a nose for the topical, no matter where it stirs in the thickets of long ago; it is the tiger's leap into the past. Such a leap, however, takes place in an arena where the ruling class gives the

*commands. The same leap in the open air of history is the dialectical leap Marx
understood as revolution.*

In a letter to Horkheimer, written in 1941 shortly after receiving a copy of the
'Theses', Adorno compared the conception of time of Thesis XIV with Paul
Tillich's '*kairos*'.[121] The Christian socialist Tillich, a close collaborator of the
Frankfurt Institute of Social Research of the twenties and thirties, contrasted
kairos – 'full' historical time, in which each moment contains a unique
opportunity, a singular constellation between relative and absolute[122] – with
chronos, formal time.

Karl Kraus's epigraph, *Ursprung ist der Ziel*, has a double meaning. From the
theological standpoint, redemption – as we have seen above – brings a return
to the lost Paradise: *tikkun, apokatastasis*, the *restitutio omnium*. And this is,
indeed, what Benjamin himself wrote in his article on Karl Kraus (1931), in
which he glosses this remark by the Viennese writer in the following terms:
'he calls the world a "wrong, deviating, circuitous way back to Paradise"
(*Irrweg, Abweg, Unweg zum Paradiese zurück*).'[123] From the political viewpoint,
the revolution is also (see Thesis IX) a return to the original Paradise. But in
Thesis XIV Benjamin is concerned with another type of relation to the past, a
relation that might be termed 'revolutionary quotation'.

How, in this context, are we to interpret the surprising comparison
between fashion and revolution? An observation in *The Arcades Project* helps
us to understand this parallel. The two apparently proceed in the same way:
while the French Revolution cites Roman antiquity, late eighteenth-century
fashion cites Greek antiquity. But the temporality of fashion is that of Hell:
while cultivating 'the absurd superstition of the new' (Paul Valéry), it is the
eternal repetition of the same, endlessly and uninterruptedly. It thus serves the
ruling classes as camouflage to conceal their 'great aversion to violent changes'
(Brecht).[124] Revolution, by contrast, is the interruption of the eternal return
and the coming of the most profound change. It is a dialectical leap, outside of
the continuum, first towards the past and then towards the future. The 'tiger's
leap into the past' consists in rescuing the heritage of the oppressed and
drawing inspiration from it in order to break into and halt the present
catastrophe.

The past contains presentness – *Jetztzeit* – a term variously translated into

English as 'now-time' and 'time of the now'. In a variant of Thesis XIV, *Jetztzeit* is defined as an explosive [*Explosivstoff*] to which historical materialism adds the fuse. The aim is to explode the continuum of history with the aid of a conception of historical time that perceives it as 'full', as charged with 'present', explosive, subversive moments.[125]

For Robespierre the Roman republic was charged with 'now-time', with that *Jetztzeit* the French republic needed in 1793. Wrenched out of its context, it becomes an explosive to be used in the battle against the monarchy, by interrupting a thousand years of royal continuity in the history of Europe. The present revolution feeds on the past, the way the tiger feeds on what he finds in the forest. But the link is a fleeting fragile one, forming only a momentary constellation that has to be seized: hence the image of the wild beast's 'leap' in time. Republican heroes, like Brutus, figure among the victims of the past, among the defeated of imperial history – that history that is written as a succession of the victory parades of the Caesars. As such, these heroes can be 'cited' by the French revolutionaries as eminently topical references.

As is well known, Marx had roundly criticized the Roman illusions of the Jacobins in *The Eighteenth Brumaire*.[126] Benjamin, who could not be unaware of that famous text, here takes the opposite stance to the founder of historical materialism. In our view he was both wrong and right to do so. He was wrong, first, because the Roman republic – a slave-holding, patrician state – could in no sense provide inspiration for the democratic ideals of 1793. And it is, indeed, amazing that Benjamin does not mention, rather than Robespierre, the example of Gracchus Babeuf, who did not 'quote' ancient Rome, but the tribunes of the Roman *plebs*. The Roman phantasmagorias of the Jacobins were indeed, as Marx had shown, an illusion. But the author of *The Eighteenth Brumaire* went too far in concluding that proletarian revolutions, unlike the bourgeois ones, could derive their poetry only from the future, and not from the past. Benjamin's profound intuitive sense of the explosive presence of the emancipatory moments of the past in the revolutionary culture of the present was right: for example, the presence of the 1793–94 Commune in the Paris Commune of 1871 and of the latter in the October Revolution of 1917. In each case – and one could cite many more examples both in Europe and in Latin America – the revolutionary uprising performed a 'tiger's leap into the past', a dialectical jump under the clear sky of history, by taking as its own an explosive moment from the past, charged with 'now-time'. The quotation of the past was not necessarily a constraint or an illusion, but could be a tremendous source of inspiration, a powerful cultural weapon in the present battle.

In another preparatory note, Benjamin contrasts the historical continuum, which is the creation of the oppressors, with tradition, which is that of the oppressed. The tradition of the oppressed – mentioned in Thesis VIII as the source of the true understanding of Fascism – is, in Benjamin's view, one of the three chief aspects of historical materialism, alongside the discontinuity of historical time and the destructive force of the working class.[127] This tradition is discontinuous: it is made up of exceptional, 'explosive' moments in the interminable succession of forms of oppression.[128] But, dialectically, it has its own continuity: to the image of the explosion that is to shatter the continuum of oppression, there corresponds, within the tradition of the oppressed, the metaphor of weaving: according to the essay on Fuchs, we must weave into 'the warp' of the present the threads of a tradition that have been lost for centuries.[129]

Thesis XV

What characterizes revolutionary classes at their moment of action is the awareness that they are about to make the continuum of history explode. The Great Revolution introduced a new calendar. The initial day of a calendar presents history in time-lapse mode [als ein historischer Zeitraffer]. *And, basically, it is this same day that keeps recurring in the guise of holidays, which are days of remembrance* [Tage des Eingedenkens]. *Thus, calendars do not measure time the way clocks do; they are monuments of a historical consciousness of which not the slightest trace has been apparent in Europe, it would seem, for the past hundred years. In the July revolution an incident occurred in which this consciousness came into its own. On the first evening of fighting, it so happened that the dials on clock towers were being fired at simultaneously and independently from several locations in Paris. An eyewitness, who may have owed his insight to the rhyme, wrote as follows:*

Qui le croirait! On dit, qu'irrités contre l'heure
De nouveaux Josués au pied de chaque tour,
Tiraient sur les cadrans pour arrêter le jour.

[Who would believe it! It is said that, incensed at the hour,
Latter-day Joshuas, at the foot of every clocktower,
Were firing on clock faces to make the day stand still.]

Revolutionary classes – that is to say, not only the proletariat, but all the oppressed of the past – are aware of blowing historical continuity apart by their action. In fact, only revolutionary action can interrupt – for a time – the triumphal procession of the victors. In peasant uprisings, medieval heretical revolts or the peasant war of the sixteenth century, this awareness took the chiliastic or apocalyptic form of 'the end of time' and the coming of the millennium: Benjamin doubtless knew his friend Ernst Bloch's book on Thomas Münzer.[130] In the French Revolution – a model that remains a constant reference for Benjamin throughout his life – this same awareness manifests itself in the introduction of a new calendar, starting from the day on which the Republic is proclaimed: 1793 was Year One of the new era.

The day a new calendar comes into force is, writes Benjamin, a *historischer Zeitraffer* – an untranslatable concept, which one of Benjamin's French translators, Pierre Missac, renders wrongly as 'le rythme de l'histoire s'accélère' and another, Maurice de Gandillac, translates literally as 'un ramasseur historique du temps'. In his own translation, Benjamin proposes: 'une sorte de raccourci historique' – i.e. a sort of historical short-cut – and he explains this as follows: the first new day incorporates into itself the whole of preceding time. Why is this the case? Perhaps because in that day, all the moments of past revolt and the full wealth of the tradition of the oppressed find themselves 'gathered up' [*ramassés*]. This is what Benjamin suggests when he observes, in one of his preparatory notes, that in the break in historical continuity – revolution – both tradition and a new beginning coincide.[131] But the expression *historischer Zeitraffer* remains enigmatic . . .

For Benjamin calendars represent the opposite of empty time: they are the expression of a historic, heterogeneous time, freighted with memory and presentness. Holidays are qualitatively distinct from other days: they are days of memory and remembrance that express a real historical consciousness. They are, as the French version has it, 'aussi bien des jours initiaux que des jours de souvenance' [as much initial days as days of remembrance],[132] the word 'initial' here referring to an emancipatory or redemptive rupture.

The Jewish calendar provides an obvious example of this, which Benjamin doubtless had in mind when writing these lines. The main holidays in that calendar are given over to the remembrance of redemptive events: the flight from Egypt (Pessach), the revolt of the Maccabees (Hanukkah), the rescue of the exiles in Persia (Purim). The imperative of memory – *Zakhor*! – is even one of the central elements of the ritual of the Jewish Passover: you are to remember your ancestors in Egypt, as though you had yourself been a slave in those times.[133]

We may, however, cite other secular holidays, such as the French 14 July or the workers' May Day – 'initial' days of popular celebration and revolutionary memory, constantly under threat from the conformism that seeks to take hold of them.

Thesis XV continues the critique of the two preceding theses against the homogeneous conception of time, but it identifies this empty temporality more precisely as *clock* time. It is the purely mechanical, automatic, quantitative, ever self-identical time of the timepiece: a time reduced to space.

Industrial-capitalist civilization has been increasingly dominated since the nineteenth century by clock time, which can be exactly measured in a strictly quantifiable way. The pages of Marx's *Capital* are filled with terrifying examples of the tyranny of the clock over workers' lives. In pre-capitalist societies, time bore qualitative significance, but, with the advance of the process of industrialization, this gradually gave way to the dominance of clock time alone.[134]

For Benjamin, historical time cannot be likened to clock time. This is a theme that goes back to his earliest writings: in the article '*Trauerspiel* and Tragedy' of 1916, he contrasts historical time, filled with messianic temporality, with the empty, mechanical time of clocks. A few years later, in his thesis on 'The Concept of Criticism in German Romanticism' (1919), he contrasts 'the qualitative temporal infinity' [*qualitative zeitliche Unendlichkeit*] of Romantic messianism with the 'empty temporal infinity' of the ideologies of progress.[135]

The conception of time proposed by Benjamin has its sources in the Jewish messianic tradition: for the Hebrews time was not an empty, abstract, linear category, but was inseparable from its content.[136] It is, however, in a way, traditional, pre-capitalist or pre-industrial cultures as a whole that retain, in their calendars and festivals, traces of the historical consciousness of time.

The act of the revolutionaries firing on the clocks during the revolution of July 1830 represents that consciousness so far as Benjamin is concerned. But here it is not the calendar clashing with the clock: it is the historical time of revolution assailing the mechanical time of the timepiece. The revolution is the attempt to arrest empty time by the irruption of qualitative, messianic time – the way that Joshua, according to the Old Testament, halted the course of the sun to gain the time he needed for victory.

In Benjamin's *Baudelaire* we also find a reference to Joshua and this aspiration to stop the march of time: 'To interrupt the course of the world – that was Baudelaire's deepest intention. The intention of Joshua.'[137] He is speaking both of a messianic and a revolutionary interruption of the catastrophic course of the world. In July 1830, the revolutionary classes – like 'latter-day Joshuas' – were still aware that their action 'blasted apart the historical continuity' of oppression.

A recent Latin-American example strikingly transposes this aspiration onto the terrain of symbolism – of protest, rather than revolution. During popular protest demonstrations – mounted by the workers' and peasants' trade union organizations and by black and indigenous movements – against the official (governmental) celebrations of the 500th anniversary of the 'discovery' of Brazil by the Portuguese navigators in 1500, a group of natives shot arrows at the clock (sponsored by the *Globo* television network) counting down the days and hours to the centenary.

THESIS XVI

The historical materialist cannot do without the notion of a present which is not a transition, but in which time takes a stand [einsteht] and has come to a standstill. For this notion defines the present in which he himself is writing history. Historicism offers the 'eternal' image of the past; historical materialism supplies a unique

Young indigenous Brazilians shooting arrows
at the official commemorative clock of the cinquecentennial
of the discovery of Brazil, April 2000.
Photograph: Carlos Eduardo: © Folha Imagem.

experience with the past. The historical materialist leaves it to others to be drained by
the whore called 'Once upon a time' in historicism's bordello. He remains in control
of his powers – man enough to blast open the continuum of history.

Pursuing his polemic against historicism, Benjamin formulates a curious allegory. We may interpret it as follows: the prostitute called 'Once upon a time', ensconced in the bordello 'Historicism', receives the victors one after another. She has no qualms about giving herself to one and then abandoning him the next moment and taking another. The succession of these victors forms the continuum of history: once upon a time there was Julius Caesar, once upon a time there was Charlemagne, once upon a time there was the Borgia pope, and so on.

By contrast, the historical materialist – who, contrary to what Benjamin implies, does not have to be of the masculine gender ('man enough') – has a

unique experience with an image of the past. The essay on Fuchs, which
contains a kind of variant of Thesis XVI, explains: that it is a matter of
perceiving – as it 'flashes' before us, to use the language of Thesis V – the
critical connection a particular fragment forms with a particular present.[138]
For example, between Walter Benjamin, in a moment of supreme danger in
1940, and Auguste Blanqui, the prisoner, the forgotten revolutionary. Or
again, in the work by Bloch mentioned above, between the revolutionary
risings in Germany in 1919–21 – that 'present in which he himself is writing
history' – and the peasant uprising inspired by Thomas Münzer. For that
constellation to be able to form, the present must, nevertheless, come to a
standstill for a moment: this is the equivalent, at the historiographical level, of
the revolutionary interruption of historical continuity.

According to the essay on Fuchs, the unique 'experience with the past'
liberates 'the immense forces bound up in historicism's "Once upon a
time"'.[139] In other words, while the conformist, pseudo-objective approach
of writers like Ranke and Sybel neutralizes and sterilizes the images of the
past, the approach of historical materialism recovers the hidden explosive
energies that are to be found in a precise moment of history. These energies,
which are those of the *Jetztzeit*, are like the spark produced by a short circuit,
enabling the continuum of history to be 'blasted apart'.

A topical example from Latin America, the Zapatist uprising of the Chiapas
in January 1994, strikingly illustrates Benjamin's ideas. There, by a 'tiger's leap
into the past', the native fighters of the EZLN liberated the explosive energies
of the legend of Emiliano Zapata[140] by wresting it from the conformism of
official history and by blasting apart the alleged historical continuity between
the Mexican Revolution of 1911–17 and the corrupt, authoritarian regime of
the PRI – the Institutional Revolutionary Party.[141]

Thesis XVII

*Historicism rightly culminates in universal history. It may be that materialist
historiography differs in method more clearly from universal history than from
any other kind. Universal history has no theoretical armature. Its procedure is
additive; it musters a mass of data to fill the homogeneous, empty time. Materialist*

historiography, on the other hand, is based on a constructive principle. Thinking involves not only the movement of thoughts, but their arrest as well. Where thinking suddenly comes to a stop in a constellation saturated with tensions, it gives that constellation a shock, by which thinking is crystallized as a monad. The historical materialist approaches a historical object only where it confronts him as a monad. In this structure he recognizes the sign of a Messianic arrest of happening, or, to put it differently, a revolutionary chance in the fight for the oppressed past. He takes cognizance of it in order to blast a specific era out of the homogeneous course of history; thus he blasts a specific life out of the era, a specific work out of the lifework. As a result of this method, the lifework is both preserved and sublated in the work, the era in the lifework and the entire course of history in the era. The nourishing fruit of what is historically understood contains time in its interior as a precious but tasteless seed.

Against the quantitative historicist conception of historical time as accumulation, Benjamin here outlines his qualitative, discontinuous conception of historical time.[142] There is a striking affinity between Benjamin's ideas here and those of Charles Péguy, an author with whom he felt a deep sense of 'oneness'.[143] According to Péguy, in *Clio* – a text published in 1931, which Benjamin might have read – the concept of time proper to the theory of progress is 'precisely the time of the savings bank and the great credit establishments . . . it is the time of interest accumulated by a capital . . . a truly homogeneous time, since it translates, transports into homogeneous calculations . . . [and] transposes into a homogeneous (mathematical) language the countless varieties of anxieties and fortunes'. Against this time of progress, 'made in the image and likeness of space', reduced to an 'absolute, infinite' line, he sets the time of memory, the time of 'organic remembrance' that is not homogeneous, but has full and empty moments.[144]

It is the task of remembrance, in Benjamin's work, to build 'constellations' linking the present and the past. These constellations, these moments wrested from empty historical continuity are monads. That is, they are concentrates of historical totality – 'full moments', as Péguy would put it.[145] The privileged moments of the past, before which the historical materialist comes to a halt, are those which constitute a messianic stop to events – like that moment in July 1830 when the insurgents fired on the clocks. These moments represent a revolutionary opportunity in the battle, today, for the oppressed past, but also, doubtless, for the oppressed present.[146]

The 'messianic arrest' is a rupture in history, but not the end of history. One of the notes explicitly asserts: 'The Messiah breaks off history; the Messiah does not appear at the end of a development.'[147] Similarly, the classless society is not the end of history, but, according to Marx, the end of prehistory – the history of the oppression and alienation of human beings.[148]

According to the preparatory notes, the universal history of historicism is false; it is a mere artificial accumulation, the way Esperanto is a false universal language. But there will one day be a true universal history, as there will be a true universal language: in the messianic world, which is the 'world of universal and integral actuality'.[149] This messianic history of delivered humanity will burn like an 'eternal lamp' that includes the totality of the past in an immense *apokatastasis*.[150]

In the letter to Gretel Adorno announcing the writing of the theses, Benjamin particularly draws her attention to the seventeenth, insofar as it reveals the connection between this document and the method of his earlier researches.[151] Benjamin's works on Baudelaire are a good example of the methodology proposed in this thesis: the aim is to discover in *Les Fleurs du mal* a monad, a crystallized ensemble of tensions that contains a historical totality. In that text, wrested from the homogeneous course of history, is preserved and gathered the whole of the poet's work, in that work the French nineteenth century, and, in this latter, the 'entire course of history'. Within Baudelaire's 'accursed' work, time lies hidden like a precious seed. Must that seed fructify in the terrain of the current class struggle to acquire its full savour?

Thesis XVIIa

In the idea of classless society, Marx secularized the idea of messianic time. And that was a good thing. It was only when the Social Democrats elevated this idea to an 'ideal' that the trouble began. The ideal was defined in Neo-Kantian doctrine as an 'infinite [unendlich] task.' And this doctrine was the school philosophy of the Social

Democratic party – from Schmidt and Stadler through Natorp and Vorländer. Once the classless society had been defined as an infinite task, the empty and homogeneous time was transformed into an anteroom, so to speak, in which one could wait for the emergence of the revolutionary situation with more or less equanimity. In reality, there is not a moment that would not carry with it its revolutionary chance – provided only that it is defined in a specific way, namely as the chance for a completely new resolution of a completely new problem [Aufgabe]. *For the revolutionary thinker, the peculiar revolutionary chance offered by every historical moment gets its warrant from the political situation. But it is equally grounded, for this thinker, in the right of entry which the historical moment enjoys vis-à-vis a quite distinct chamber of the past, one which up to that point has been closed and locked. The entrance into this chamber coincides in a strict sense with political action, and it is by means of such entry that political action, however destructive, reveals itself as messianic. (Classless society is not the final goal of historical progress but its frequently miscarried, ultimately* [endlich] *achieved interruption.)*

The concept of secularization employed by Benjamin in this thesis is, probably, a reference to Carl Schmitt's *Political Theology* (1922), according to which 'all significant concepts of the modern theory of the state are secularized theological concepts'. Schmitt is, admittedly, more interested in counter-revolutionary philosophies of the state, but he also formulates some more general hypotheses that might have interested Benjamin. He writes, for example, that 'the exception in jurisprudence is analogous to the miracle in theology'.[152] However, as Jacob Taubes has very ably demonstrated, secularization for Schmitt is not a positive concept. On the contrary, 'for him it represents the devil'. Schmitt's aim is to show that secularization leads the juridical theory of the state into an impasse because it is ignorant of the foundation, the roots of its own concepts.[153]

This is not Benjamin's standpoint: for him, secularization is both legitimate and necessary – on condition that the subversive energy of the messianic remains present, even if as an occult force (like theology in the materialist chess player). What is to be criticized, insists Benjamin, is not secularization as such, but a specific form, that of Social Democratic Neo-Kantianism, which turned the messianic idea into an ideal, an 'infinite task'. Those chiefly implicated in this were the Marburg University group of philosophers to which Alfred Stadler and Paul Natorp – two of the authors mentioned in the thesis – belonged, together with Hermann Cohen.

We find here a striking similarity with ideas developed by the young Scholem in his unpublished notebooks from the years 1918–19. He rails there, with incredible virulence, against the fraudulent imitation of the Jewish messianic tradition the Neo-Kantian Marburg School has, in his view, perpetrated:

> The messianic realm and mechanical time have produced, in the heads of Enlightenment thinkers (*Aufklärer*), the – bastardized, accursed – idea of Progress. Because, if one is an *Aufklärer* . . . the prospect of messianic times must necessarily be warped into Progress . . . This is where the most fundamental errors of the Marburg School are to be found: the distortion . . . of everything into an infinite task in the sense of Progress. This is the most pitiful interpretation prophecy has ever had to bear.[154]

We may wonder whether Benjamin did not have these ideas in mind when he wrote the 'Theses' of 1940 – unless it was Scholem who was inspired to write this by his discussions with his friend in 1916–19.

Benjamin reproaches Neo-Kantian-inspired Social Democracy, above all, for its *attentisme*, the Olympian calm with which it awaits, comfortably installed in empty and homogeneous time like a courtier in the anteroom, the inescapable advent of the 'revolutionary situation' – which, of course, will never come.

The alternative he proposes is both historical and political, and it is both of these things inseparably. It starts out from the hypothesis that each moment has its revolutionary potentialities. And in it an open conception of history as human praxis, rich in unexpected possibilities and able to produce something new, stands opposed to any kind of teleological doctrine that trusts in the 'laws of history' or in the gradual accumulation of reforms on the safe and sure path of infinite Progress.

This political action – which, like any revolutionary praxis, has a destructive dimension to it – is, at the same time, a messianic interruption of history and a 'leap into the past': it has the magical power to gain entry (*Schlüsselmacht*: literally, 'key power') to a 'chamber' (*Gemach*) that has until now been locked away (*verschlossenes*), to an event that has until now been forgotten. We find here once again the deep, close, messianic unity between revolutionary action in the present and the intervention of memory in a determinate moment of the past.[155] The rediscovery, with the rise of the feminist movement of the 1970s, of the forgotten, 'locked-away' texts of Olympe de Gouges – the author of pamphlets denouncing slavery and of the 'Declaration of the Rights of Woman' (1791), who was guillotined under the Terror in 1793 – is a striking example of this. For a century and a half, the official historiography of the French Revolution had forgotten this tragic, subversive figure.

The concept of the classless society – with all its messianic charge – occupies a central place in this thesis – and, indeed, in the whole of the document. It is a crucial political and historical reference point, serving as a goal for the struggle of the oppressed and a criterion by which to judge systems of oppression past and present. As one of Benjamin's notes says, 'Without some sort of assay of the classless society, there is only a historical accumulation of the past. To this extent, every concept of the present participates in the concept of Judgement Day.'[156]

THESIS XVIII

'In relation to the history of all organic life on earth,' writes a modern biologist, 'the paltry fifty-millennia history of homo sapiens equates to something like two seconds at the close of a twenty-four-hour day. On this scale, the history of civilized mankind would take up one-fifth of the last second of the last hour.' Now-time, which, as a model of messianic time, comprises the entire history of mankind in a tremendous abbreviation, coincides exactly with the figure which the history of mankind describes in the universe.

Jetztzeit, 'now-time' or 'the present', is defined in this instance as the 'model' or foreshadowing of messianic time, of the 'eternal lamp', of the true history of mankind. To explain the concept of the messianic arrest of events, Benjamin refers, in one of the preparatory notes, to Henri Focillon, who spoke of the 'brief perfectly balanced instant of complete possession of forms'.[157] The messianic monad is a brief instant of complete possession of history prefiguring the whole, the saved totality, the universal history of liberated humanity – in a word, the history of salvation (*Heilsgeschichte*) to which one of the notes refers.[158]

As is well-known, the monad – a concept that is Neoplatonist in origin – is, in Leibniz, a reflection of the entire universe. Examining this concept in *The Arcades Project*, Benjamin defines it as 'the crystal of the total event'.[159]

Once again here we come upon the idea of 'abbreviation' (*Abbreviatur*), the enigmatic *historischer Zeitraffer*. On this question, an interesting line of argument is suggested by Giorgio Agamben. The messianic time which 'compris[es] all of history' (Benjamin actually uses the word '*zusammenfasst*': literally 'seizes together') is reminiscent of the Christian concept of *anakephalaiosis* that appears in one of Paul's epistles to the Ephesians: 'He might gather together in one all things in Christ' (Eph 1: 10), which, in Luther's translation, becomes: '*alle ding zusamen verfasset würde in Christo*'.[160]

Jetztzeit comprises all the messianic moments of the past, the whole tradition of the oppressed is concentrated, as a redemptive power, in the present moment, the moment of the historian – or of the revolutionary.[161]

In this way, the Spartakist rising of January 1919 sees a unique constellation formed with the *Jetztzeit* of the ancient slave rising. But this monad, this brief moment, is an abbreviation of the whole history of mankind as the history of the struggle of the oppressed. Moreover, as a messianic interruption of events, as a brief instant of liberation, this act of revolt prefigures the universal history of saved humanity.

We might, then, regard Thesis IX as a stunning example of an immense abbreviation of the history of mankind up to this point, a crystal encapsulating the totality of the catastrophic events that constitute the thread of that history. But in that image the only foreshadowing of redemption is negative: the impossibility, for the angel of history, to 'awaken the dead, and make whole what has been smashed'.

Thesis A

Historicism contents itself with establishing a causal nexus among various moments in history. But no state of affairs having causal significance is for that very reason historical. It became historical posthumously, as it were, through events that may be

separated from it by thousands of years. The historian who proceeds from this
consideration ceases to tell the sequence of events like the beads of a rosary. He grasps
the constellation into which his own era has entered, along with a very specific earlier
one. Thus, he establishes a conception of the present as now-time shot through with
splinters of messianic time.

It is the constellation formed by a present situation and a past event that makes
the latter a historical fact. To give an example that was dear to Benjamin – and
in which 'thousands of years' certainly separate the historian from the
event in question – the discovery by Engels (drawing on the works of
Morgan) of the primitive community as an important historical reality, is
inseparable from the modern struggle for the new community – the classless
society.

This approach breaks with the blinkered determinism of the historicists and
their linear-evolutionary vision of the 'course of events': it uncovers a
privileged connection between past and present, which is not that of causality
or 'progress' – for which the archaic community is merely a 'backward' stage
that is of no interest in the present – but a 'secret pact' in which 'the spark of
hope' shines out.

The 'splinters (*Splitter*) of messianic time' are the moments of revolt, the
brief instants that save a past moment, while effecting a fleeting interruption
of historical continuity, a break in the heart of the present.[62] As fragmentary,
partial redemptions, they prefigure and herald the possibility of universal
salvation.[63]

These 'splinters' refer, then, to the imminent or potential presence of
the messianic era in history which will be evoked in the last of the theses.
This is an idea Benjamin had carried with him since youth, as witness this
astonishing passage from Scholem's unpublished notebooks of 1917, in
which we see Scholem, who, where Judaism was concerned, regarded
himself as his friend's mentor, refer to Benjamin as an – almost canonical –
source:

In the idea of the messianic kingdom one finds the greatest image of
history, on which infinitely profound relationships between religion and
ethics are built. Walter said once: The messianic kingdom is always there.

This insight contains *the greatest* truth – but only in a sphere which, to my knowledge, no one since the prophets has attained to.[164]

Qualitative time, studded [*constellé*] with messianic splinters, stands radically opposed to the empty flow of the purely quantitative time of historicism and 'progressism'. We are, here, in the rupture between messianic redemption and the ideology of progress, at the heart of the constellation formed by the conceptions of history of Benjamin, Scholem and Franz Rosenzweig, who draw on the Jewish religious tradition to contest the model of thought that is common to Christian theodicy, the Enlightenment and the Hegelian philosophy of history. By abandoning the Western teleological model, we pass from a time of necessity to a time of possibilities, a random time, open at any moment to the unforeseeable irruption of the new.[165] But, from the political standpoint, we are also on the central strategic axis of the reconstruction of Marxism attempted by Benjamin.

Thesis B

The soothsayers who queried time and learned what it had in store certainly did not experience it as either homogeneous or empty. Whoever keeps this in mind will perhaps get an idea of how past times were experienced in remembrance – namely, in just this way. We know that the Jews were prohibited from inquiring into the future: the Torah and the prayers instructed them in remembrance. This disenchanted the future, which holds sway over all those who turn to soothsayers for enlightenment. This does not imply, however, that for the Jews the future became homogeneous, empty time. For every second was the small gateway in time through which the Messiah might enter.

First, Benjamin rejects the approach of those who turn to soothsayers for information, because they are enslaved by the future: if you think you know the future, you are doomed to passivity, to waiting for the inevitable to happen – and this remark applies equally to that modern form of the ancient oracle, the 'scientific predictions' of historical materialism transformed into an 'automaton'.[166]

The Messiah before the Strait Gate at Jerusalem. Sixteenth-century Haggadah.

Jewish tradition, by contrast, demands the remembrance of the past – the biblical imperative: *Zakhor*.[167] But, as Yossef Hayim Yerushalmi observes, what the Jews seek is 'not the historicity of the past, but its eternal contemporaneity'.[168] Similarly, the revolutionary, in his present action, draws his inspiration and his fighting spirit from remembrance and in that way escapes the baleful spell of the guaranteed, predictable, assured future offered by the modern 'soothsayers'.

Certainly the most striking passage in this thesis, and the one that has given rise to most debate and comment, is its conclusion. What we must emphasize, first of all, is that it is not a matter of awaiting the Messiah, as in the dominant tradition of rabbinical Judaism, but of bringing about his coming. In the preparatory notes, after comparing the messianic interruption with certain ideas of Henri Focillon, Benjamin quotes the following passage from the art critic on the 'current [French] expression *"faire date"'*: 'It is not a question of breaking quietly in on chronology, but of bursting suddenly in on the moment.'[169] Benjamin belongs to the dissident tradition of those who were known as the *dohakei haketz*, those who 'hasten the end of time'.[170]

This theme was surely inspired, almost word for word, by a work which was, from the 1920s onwards, one of his main Jewish sources, Franz Rosenzweig's *Star of Redemption* (1921). For Rosenzweig, 'Every moment can be the last. That is what makes it eternal . . .' But it is not a question of waiting: 'The future is not a future without this anticipation and the inner compulsion for it, without this "wish to bring about the Messiah before his time" . . . without these, it is only a past distended endlessly . . .' This conception stands opposed, of course, to all doctrines of progress: 'Thus the real idea of progress resists nothing so strongly as the possibility that the "ideal goal" could and should be reached, perhaps in the next moment, or even in this very moment.'[171]

Historical remembrance and subversive praxis, heretical messianism and revolutionary voluntarism – Rosenzweig and Blanqui are combined in this *dialectical image* of the coming of the Messiah through the 'small gateway' [*die kleine Pforte*].

For Rolf Tiedemann, Benjamin's proposition here is an impotent decree that leaves out of account any analysis of reality. It is, he argues, more of the order of anarchism and putschism than of Marxist sobriety.[172]

Honoré Daumier, *The Riot*.

Admittedly, from the 1929 article on Surrealism onwards, Benjamin set it as one of his objectives to add a measure of the intoxication (*Rausch*) and anarchist spontaneity the Surrealists embodied to Marxist sobriety and discipline. But his objective was not so much to 'decree' revolution as to plead for a conception of history as open process, not determined in advance, in which surprises, unexpected strokes of good fortune and unforeseen opportunities may appear at any moment. It is not so much a question of 'putschism' here, as of being able to grasp the fleeting moment in which revolutionary action is possible – as, with great presence of mind, the anarchists of the FAI-CNT and the Marxists of the POUM did in Catalonia in the summer of 1936 (to cite only one example which Benjamin doubtless knew, even if he does not seem to have grasped the entire significance of it at the time) by opposing the Fascist uprising through force of arms and by establishing a genuine socialist and libertarian 'state of exception', though alas it was short-lived. But what does the tradition of the oppressed consist in, if not in the discontinuous series of rare moments in which the chain of domination has been broken?

2

The Opening-up of History

In the history of twentieth-century ideas, Benjamin's 'Theses' seem to represent a detour, a mere byway beside the great highways of thought. But whereas the latter are carefully marked out, clearly signposted, and lead to duly charted stopping-off points, Benjamin's little path goes to an unknown destination. The 1940 'Theses' represent a kind of philosophical manifesto, in the form of dialectical images and allegories rather than abstract syllogisms, for *the opening-up of history*. That is, for a conception of the historical process that opens onto a dizzying field of possibilities, a vast branching structure of alternatives, without, however, falling into the illusion of absolute liberty: the 'objective conditions' are also conditions of possibility.

That conception stands explicitly on the ground of the Marxist tradition – 'historical materialism' – which Benjamin wishes to wrench from the bureaucratic conformism that threatens it as much as, if not more than, does the enemy. As we have seen, his relation to the Marxian heritage is highly selective and involves the abandonment of – rather than the explicit critique of, or a direct 'settling of accounts' with – all the moments in the works of Marx and Engels that have served as references for the positivistic/evolutionary readings of Marxism in terms of irresistible progress, 'the laws of history' and 'natural necessity'. Benjamin's reading stands in direct contradiction to this idea of inevitability, which from the *Communist Manifesto* onwards haunts certain texts by Marx and Engels: 'What the bourgeoisie . . .

produces, above all, are its own grave-diggers. Its fall and the victory of the proletariat are equally inevitable'.[1] Nothing is further from Benjamin's approach than the belief, suggested by certain passages in *Capital*, in a historical necessity of a 'natural' kind (*Naturnotwendigkeit*).[2]

The work of Marx and Engels doubtless has unresolved tensions running through it between a certain fascination with the natural scientific model and a dialectical-critical approach, between faith in the organic and quasi-natural maturation of the social process and the strategic vision of revolutionary action that seizes an exceptional moment. These tensions explain the diversity of Marxisms that were to dispute the Marxian heritage after the death of its founders.[3] In the 'Theses' of 1940, Benjamin ignores ideas at the former end of the Marxian spectrum and takes his inspiration from the latter.

Why does Benjamin prefer to attack Social Democratic epigones rather than contest certain of the writings of Marx and Engels themselves which made those interpretations possible? We may assume that there were several – not necessarily contradictory – reasons for this attitude: (a) the conviction that the real Marx lies elsewhere and the positivist moments are secondary; (b) the political option of setting Marx himself against his epigones, who have in any case diluted or traduced his message; (c) the desire, following the example of his masters Lukács and Korsch, to state his reading of historical materialism in a positive mode, rather than critically review the writings of the founders.

Though no direct criticisms of Marx and Engels are to be found in the 'Theses' themselves, they do figure here and there in the associated notes – for example, in the note on revolution as the locomotive of history, which calls into question, through that image, the entire vision of progress as a linear, irresistible process.[4] More important is the remark on the productive forces as the chief criterion of progress: this is actually a point of major significance, which occupies a crucial place in the work of the fathers of modern socialism and which largely fuelled the economistic interpretations of the Second International and Stalinist productivism. But the question remains at the level of a programmatic proposal and Benjamin does not go into it more deeply.

The 'recasting' of historical materialism in the 'Theses' also involves, of course, a selective – and heterodox – reappropriation of the Marxian themes that seem to him essential to his undertaking: the state as class domination, the class struggle, the social revolution and the utopia of a classless society.

Materialism itself, revised by theology, is incorporated into his theoretical system. Benjamin takes his inspiration from texts like the 1844 Manuscripts, the historical writings on the Revolution of 1848–50 or the Paris Commune, and the 'Critique of the Gotha Programme' – all copiously cited and commented on in *The Arcades Project*.

The result is a reworking, a critical reformulation of Marxism, integrating messianic, romantic, Blanquist, libertarian and Fourierist 'splinters' into the body of historical materialism. Or, rather, it is the fabrication, on the basis of the fusion of all these materials, of a new heretical Marxism, radically different from all the – orthodox or dissident – variants of his time. A 'messianic Marxism' which could not but arouse, as Benjamin himself had predicted, perplexity and incomprehension. But also, and above all, *a Marxism of unpredictability*: if history is open, if 'the new' is possible, this is because the future is not known in advance; the future is not the ineluctable result of a given historical evolution, the necessary and predictable outcome of the 'natural' laws of social transformation, the inevitable fruit of economic, technical or scientific progress – or, worse still, the continuation, in ever more perfected forms, of the same, of what already exists, of actually existing modernity, of the current economic and social structures.[5]

What is the meaning today, at the dawn of the twenty-first century, sixty years after Benjamin's death, of this opening-up of history?

First, on the cognitive level, it throws light on a new horizon for thought: the search for a dialectical rationality which, shattering the smooth mirror of uniform temporality, rejects the pitfalls of 'scientific prediction' of the positivist type and brings within its purview the *clinamen* rich in possibilities, the *kairos* pregnant with strategic opportunities.[6]

Unpredictability is, admittedly, only relative: it seems undeniable that a certain number of twentieth-century predictions have, more or less, come to pass. There remains, nonetheless, in the course of historical events, an irreducible core of the unexpected that lies beyond the most rigorous 'calculations of probability'. This is not merely a result of the limitations inherent in the methods of the social sciences, but arises from the very nature of human praxis. Unlike lunar eclipses or Halley's comet, the outcome of the historical action of individuals and social groups remains, to a substantial degree, unpredictable.

There is nothing mystical or 'irrational' in this observation: it flows from the very nature of politics as a collective, plural human activity, which, though admittedly conditioned by the existing social and economic structures, is capable of exceeding, transforming or overturning them by creating something new. Whether this irreducible dimension is described as 'the subjective factor', 'voluntarism', 'the freedom of the subject', 'the autonomy of social actors' or 'the human project', the fact remains that political action defies any attempt to analyse it as a mere function of structures or, even worse, as the outcome of the 'scientific laws' of history, economics or society.[7] If no one in June 1789 foresaw the fall of the Bastille – or, even less, the execution of the king and the proclamation of the Republic – this is not because contemporaries lacked adequate instruments of scientific knowledge, as a particularly dogmatic positivism might claim, but because these events were, as innovative historical acts, essentially unpredictable.[8]

If we take seriously the tragic aspect of Benjamin's vision of history, this power of innovative political action is not necessarily a source of optimism: it may perfectly well lead, as the history of the twentieth century abundantly illustrates, to terrifying results.[9]

From the political point of view, open history means, then, taking into account the possibility – though not the inevitability – of *catastrophes* on the one hand and great *emancipatory* movements on the other. This is far from obvious today: are we not living in a pacified age, infinitely far removed from the years of war and revolution of the first half of the last century?

Many works on Walter Benjamin published in recent years assert, or suggest, that this fascinating author belongs to a tragic historical conjuncture that is now past and gone. The philosophical problematics that correspond to current social and historical reality are said to be more of the order of the resolution of conflict by the democratic, rational procedures of communicative action (Habermas) or in terms of the postmodern relativism of language games (Lyotard). We have, it is said, a choice between perfecting modernity by discursive rationality or going beyond it into postmodernity by putting an end to grand narratives.

Now, although it is clear that history does not repeat itself and our age bears little resemblance to the 1930s, it seems difficult to believe that, in the light of the experience of the end of the twentieth century, wars, ethnic conflicts and massacres belong only to a distant past. Or that racism, xenophobia and even fascism no longer represent a danger for democracy. To these threats of catastrophe which echo past disasters, we should add other, newer ones: for example, the possibility of a major ecological disaster putting the very survival of the human race in danger – a form of destruction wrought by the 'storm we call progress', which Benjamin, in spite of his critical thinking on the domination/exploitation of nature, could not foresee. Or, alternatively, the possibility of new, unpredictable forms of barbarism that do not replicate those of the past, which may be produced during the coming century, as long as modern societies remain subject to relations of inequality and exclusion.

Contrary to what the reassuring discourse of the present *doxa* claims, Benjamin's fire alarm retains its currency to a striking extent: catastrophe is possible – if not, indeed, probable – *unless* . . . Though formulated in the style of the biblical prophets, Benjamin's pessimistic predictions are conditional: there is a danger of this happening, *if* . . .

And this means that the worst is not unavoidable. History remains open; it has other – revolutionary, emancipatory and/or utopian – possibilities to it. Benjamin helps us to give utopia back its negative force by the break with any teleological determinism and any ideal model of society that maintains the illusion of an end to conflict and hence to history. The conception of utopia suggested by the 1940 'Theses' has the advantage of being formulated predominantly in the negative: a class*less* society *without* domination, in the strong sense of *Herrschaft*: a heteronomous power that imposes its rules and is beyond any democratic control. This revolutionary aspiration is directed not only against the authoritarian wielding of power through the cunning and violence of the governing classes, oligarchies or elites, but also against the impersonal, abstract and reified ('fetishistic') domination of capital, commodities and bureaucratic apparatuses.

Benjamin refers predominantly to the emancipation of the oppressed classes, but his general criticism of oppression and his appeal to see history from the standpoint of the victims – of all victims – give his project a more universal scope. Similarly, his criticisms of the exploitation of nature, in spite of their allusive and incomplete character, break sharply with the positivist, scientistic, productivist culture of the hegemonic schools of thought on the

Left. They find a surprising topicality in the aspirations of some of the new internationalist movements against neo-liberal globalization, and in social ecology's project of reconstructing a harmonious equilibrium between human societies and nature – eminently universal issues inasmuch as they concern humanity in its entirety.

Walter Benjamin was far from being a 'utopian' thinker. Unlike his friend Ernst Bloch, he was preoccupied less with the 'principle of hope' and more with the urgent necessity of organizing pessimism; interested less in the 'radiant future' and more in the imminent dangers looming over humanity. He is not far from a tragic world-view of the kind one finds in the youthful essays of Lukács or in the work of Pascal, as analysed after the fashion of Lukács by Lucien Goldmann: the deep sense of an unbridgeable abyss between the authentic values one believes in and empirical reality.[10]

However, as we have seen in the preceding pages, a fragile utopian dimension – because it is entirely shot through with romantic melancholy and the tragic sense of defeat – is present in his work. Against the dominant tendency in the historic Left, which has often reduced socialism to economic objectives of concern to the industrial working class – itself reduced to its male, white, 'national', stably employed fraction – Benjamin's thinking enables us to conceive a revolutionary project with a general mission to emancipate.

This is what is needed if we are to be able to face up to the ethical and political demands of our time and re-fire the ambition – which is doubtless excessive, but what use to human action would a measured, moderate, mediocre utopia be? – of putting an end to the domination of one class over another, one sex over the other, one nation over another and human beings over nature. This is a universal objective which takes its inspiration from the unfulfilled promise of 1789: Liberty, Equality and Fraternity – or, rather, Solidarity, since sisters are included as much as brothers. These are revolutionary values, which contain, as Ernst Bloch emphasized, a utopian excess that goes beyond the narrow, petty limits of bourgeois society. Utopian universality – which is subversive (*umwälzende*) in its aim, following the definition Karl Mannheim gives of the concept of utopia – stands opposed, term for term, to the ideological pseudo-universality that regards the present status quo as the achieved human universal.[11]

So far as a different future is concerned, the current dominant discourse expresses a categorically *closed* conception of history. According to that discourse, since the fall of 'actually existing socialism' and the triumph of the Western/Atlantic system, we can affirm once and for all the end of utopias, the end of any possibility of changing the civilizational paradigm. Our age is the first for a very long time – since the beginning of the nineteenth century? – to have dared quite simply to proclaim 'the end of history': Francis Fukuyama's famous essay merely dresses up in pseudo-Hegelian language the deeply anchored conviction of the dominant elites regarding the durability of their economic and social system, which is seen not merely as infinitely superior to any other, but as the only one possible, as the last horizon of history, the ultimate, definitive destination in the long march of humanity. This does not mean that, for the current hegemonic discourse – scientific, technical, economic, social and cultural – progress is not continuing. On the contrary, it will see some tremendous advances, but it will do so within the framework, now fixed once and for all, of the industrial-capitalist economy and the existing, so-called 'liberal democratic' system. To sum it up, *'le progrès dans l'ordre'*, as Auguste Comte had so well 'predicted'.

This problematic finds striking expression in a fine text published some years ago by Georg Lukács's former disciple Agnes Heller. She observes that, for many centuries, humanity's utopian quest took the form of a sea voyage, of a ship setting sail for an island of contentment. In the nineteenth century, the image of the train came to predominate – the metaphor of the locomotive advancing, at increasing speed, towards the radiant future, towards the station 'Utopia', sweeping away all the obstacles in its path. In fact, asserts the Hungarian philosopher, we have to say goodbye to the idea of a utopia situated in an imaginary future or place: the journey to the promised land is an illusion. We have, in fact, already reached the end of our journey, which is the modernity in which we live. The metaphor that corresponds to this historical reality is that of a magnificent, spacious railway station, into which we are settled and from which we shall not depart: we must abandon the dangerous myth of an *elsewhere* and – especially – of an *otherwise*.[12]

As we have seen, Walter Benjamin also uses the allegory of the train, but in order to invert it dialectically: the train of history is heading for the abyss; revolution is the interruption of this catastrophe-bound journey. In his open

conception of history, different outcomes are possible, including revolutionary action – which appears more as a desperate attempt to prevent the
worst from happening, than as the product of the 'maturing of objective
conditions'.[13]

Benjamin often refers to the oppressed classes as the subject of emancipatory praxis. Now, in the note on the train, he speaks of the whole of
humanity 'activat[ing] the emergency brake'.[14] This universalist approach –
which doubtless stands opposed to the particularist corporatism of a certain
political/trade-unionist ideology, though not necessarily to the decisive role
of social classes – enables us to rethink social emancipation and the abolition
of domination from the viewpoint of the multiplicity of collective or
individual subjects.

For an open conception of history, emancipatory/revolutionary action is
of the order, in the last analysis, of a kind of wager. The word does not appear
anywhere in Benjamin, but it corresponds exactly to the spirit of the 1940
'Theses'. According to Lucien Goldmann – who does not seem to have been
familiar with Benjamin's writings – the Marxian utopia of an authentic
human community is of the order of a Pascalian wager: it is the engagement
of individuals – or social groups – in an action that involves risk, the danger of
failure, the hope of success, but to which one commits one's life. Any wager
of this type is motivated by trans-individual values, whether these are
immanent and secular, as in the Marxist wager on the achievement of the
socialist community, or transcendental and sacred, as in Pascal's wager on the
existence of God, and is not susceptible of scientific proof or factual
demonstration.[15]

Of course, emancipatory social and historical actors behaving in accordance
with this wager take into consideration all the objective conditions and order
their praxis as a function of the real contradictions of society; but they know
the success of their struggle is not guaranteed. That struggle is inspired by an
ethical imperative, a categorical imperative which the young Marx formulated as follows: one must struggle 'to overthrow all conditions in which man
is a debased, enslaved, neglected and contemptible being'.[16] It is this universal
moral exigency – to fight for the abolition of unjust and inhuman social
systems – that motivates their commitment, irrespective of the chances of
victory and whatever the 'scientific' predictions of the future.[17] This un-

certainty, far from leading to passivity or resignation, provides a powerful motivation for greater activity, since, within the limits laid down by the objective conditions, the future will be what we make of it.[18]

It is not just the future and the present that remain open in the Benjaminian interpretation of historical materialism, but also the past. And this means, first of all, that the historical variant that triumphed was not the only possible one. Against the history written by the victors, the celebration of the *fait accompli*, the historical one-way streets and the 'inevitability' of the victory of those who triumphed, we must come back to this essential proposition: each present opens onto a multiplicity of possible futures.[19] In every historical conjuncture, there were alternatives, which were not doomed to fail from the outset: the exclusion of women from citizenship in the French Revolution was not unavoidable; the rise to power of a Stalin or a Hitler was not (like the rise of Brecht's Arturo Ui) irresistible; and the decision to drop the atom bomb on Hiroshima had nothing inevitable about it. We could add many other examples to this list.

The opening-up of the past means also that the so-called 'judgements of history' have nothing definitive or unchangeable about them. The future may reopen 'closed' historical cases, may 'rehabilitate' misrepresented victims, revive defeated hopes and aspirations, rediscover forgotten battles or battles regarded as 'utopian', 'anachronistic' or 'running against the grain of progress'. In this case, the opening-up of the past and the opening-up of the future are intimately linked.

There is no shortage of examples of such a linkage. We have only to think of the rediscovery after 1968 of the heretical thinking of the Saint-Simonian feminist Claire Demar, whose tremendously subversive work, *Ma loi d'avenir* (1834) had been almost entirely forgotten for a century and a half. I say 'almost', because the book had not escaped the watchful Walter Benjamin, who, in his *Arcades Project*, shows great sympathy for Claire Demar's 'anthropological materialism' and her critiques of patriarchy, springing to her defence against the 'sordid' attacks of the representatives of 'the established bourgeoisie'.[20]

The work of the historian E. P. Thompson on the making of the English working class is another striking manifestation of the 'reopening of the past'. He lays his cards on the table in the Preface with a statement that was to serve as emblem and shibboleth for a new school of social history: 'I am seeking to rescue the poor stockinger, the Luddite cropper, the "obsolete" hand-loom weaver, the "utopian" artisan, and even the deluded follower of Joanna Southcott, from the enormous condescension of posterity'. The ironic quotation marks around 'utopian' and 'obsolete' represent in themselves an entire programme that implicitly challenges the categories of a dominant historiography steeped in the ideology of linear, beneficent, inevitable progress.[21] Without acritically 'idealizing' these figures from the past, this emphasis on the human and social significance of their struggle brings out the limitations of the 'progressist', 'modernizing' visions of history, which conflate the successful with the possible and end up subscribing, willy-nilly, to the grand narrative of the victors of the Industrial Revolution.

Whether we are looking at the past or the future, the opening-up of history in Walter Benjamin is inseparable from an ethical, social and political decision to support the victims of oppression and those who fight that oppression. The future of this uncertain fight and the forms it takes will no doubt be inspired or marked by past efforts: they will be none the less novel for that – and wholly impossible to predict.

NOTES

Introduction

1. H. Arendt, *Men in Dark Times* (San Diego, New York and London: Harcourt, Brace, 1995), pp. 155–6, 176.
2. G. Scholem: 'Benjamin was a philosopher. He was a philosopher at every stage and in all fields of his activity. It seems that he writes mainly on the themes of literature and art and sometimes also on subjects on the border line between literature and politics, but rarely on questions conventionally regarded and accepted as themes of pure philosophy. But in all these fields his impetus comes from the experience of the philosopher.' *Walter Benjamin und sein Engel* (Frankfurt: Suhrkamp, 1983), pp. 14–15.
3. Letter quoted by Gary Smith in 'Thinking through Benjamin: An introductory essay', *Benjamin: Philosophy, Aesthetics, History* (Chicago: University of Chicago Press, 1989), pp. viii–ix. The date of the letter is not mentioned, but from the context it must be 1967.
4. Among the exceptions are: Daniel Bensaïd, *Walter Benjamin. Sentinelle messianique à la gauche du possible* (Paris: Plon, 1990); Stéphane Mosès, *L'Ange de l'histoire: Rosenzweig, Benjamin, Scholem* (Paris: Seuil, 1992); Jeanne-Marie Gagnebin, *Histoire et narration chez Walter Benjamin* (Paris: L'Harmattan, 1994); Arno Münster, *Progrès et catastrophe, Walter Benjamin et l'histoire* (Paris: Éditions Kimé, 1996).
5. In an article published in *Le Monde*, 31 May 1969.
6. J. Habermas, 'L'actualité de W. Benjamin', *Revue d'esthétique*, 1, p. 112; *The Philosophical Discourse of Modernity*, trans. Frederick Lawrence (Cambridge: Polity Press, 1987), pp. 11–16.

7. Jean-François Lyotard, *The Postmodern Condition* (Manchester: Manchester University Press, 1984).

8. A postmodern academic with an interest in Walter Benjamin acknowledges that his idea of a loss or incompletion in the past that has to be overcome in the future 'precludes any conception of the present as agonistic' and is, therefore, in contradiction with the postmodern approach. See Andrew Benjamin, 'Tradition and Experience: Walter Benjamin's "On Some Motifs in Baudelaire"', *The Problems of Modernity: Adorno and Benjamin* (London: Routledge, 1991), pp. 137–9.

9. *Men in Dark Times*, p. 201.

10. G. Scholem and Theodor W. Adorno (eds), *The Correspondence of Walter Benjamin 1910–1940* (Chicago and London: University of Chicago Press, 1994), pp. 360, 365.

11. W. Benjamin, *The Arcades Project* (Cambridge, MA: Harvard University Press, 1999), p. 462.

12. W. Benjamin, *Correspondence*, p. 572. For Benjamin's article on Goethe's work, see 'Goethe's Elective Affinities', *Selected Writings,* vol. 1, 1913–1926 (Cambridge, MA/London: The Belknap Press of the University of Harvard Press, 1996), pp. 297–360. Hereafter *SW*.

13. L. Goldmann, *Lukács and Heidegger. Towards a New Philosophy* (London: Routledge & Kegan Paul, 1977).

14. Stéphane Mosès is right to stress the exceptional continuity in Benjamin's intellectual itinerary: it is not so much a case of evolution, he writes, as of stratification. But he nonetheless recognizes the importance of the Marxist turning point, after which can be seen a new distrust of the abstract, irresponsible character of a purely aesthetic view of history. See *L'Ange de l'histoire: Rosenzweig, Benjamin, Scholem* (Paris: Seuil, 1992), pp. 145–6.

15. For a more detailed discussion of the concept of Romanticism, I refer to my work – in collaboration with Robert Sayre – *Romanticism against the Tide of Modernity* (Durham, NC: Duke University Press, 2001).

16. W. Benjamin, 'Romantik' (1913), *Gesammelte Schriften*, ed. Rolf Tiedemann and Hermann Schweppenhäuser (Frankfurt: Suhrkamp, 1974–91), II, 1, p. 46. Hereafter *GS*.

17. W. Benjamin, 'Dialog über die Religiosität der Gegenwart', 1913, *GS*, II, 1, pp. 16–34.

18. W. Benjamin, 'The Life of Students', *SW*, 1, p. 43.

19. Ibid., p. 37.

20. W. Benjamin, 'The Concept of Criticism in German Romanticism', *SW*, 1, p. 185.

21. Ibid., p. 168.

22. W. Benjamin, 'Theological-Political Fragment', *SW*, 3, p. 305.

23. Ibid., pp. 305–6. Cf. Rosenzweig, *The Star of Redemption*, trans. by William W. Hallo (London: Routledge & Kegan Paul, 1971), p. 286.

24. W. Benjamin, 'Bücher, die lebendig geblieben sind', *GS*, III, p. 171. I have been influenced here in the translation of the German by Michael Löwy's French translation [Trans.].

25. See Arno Münster's splendid book *Progrès et catastrophe, Walter Benjamin et l'histoire. Réflexions sur l'itinéraire philosophique d'un marxisme 'mélancolique'* (Paris: Éditions Kimé, 1996), p. 64. After Benjamin's death, this posture will be taken over – with some nuances and reservations – by the critical theory of the Frankfurt School.

26. W. Benjamin, *One-Way Street* (London: Verso, 1997), p. 80. There is a striking affinity between this text and the ideas of a Marxist revolutionary whom Benjamin no doubt knew, even if he does not quote her: namely, Rosa Luxemburg. In her pamphlet, *The Crisis of Social Democracy* ('the Junius Pamphlet'), she formulated the famous slogan 'Socialism or Barbarism' that broke with the European Left's illusions of linear progress and an assured future.

27. W. Benjamin, 'Surrealism. The Last Snapshot of the European Intelligentsia' (1929), *SW*, 2, p. 216.

28. Pierre Naville, *La Révolution et les intellectuels* (Paris: Gallimard, 1965), pp. 75–6, 110–17.

29. W. Benjamin, *SW*, 2, pp. 216–17.

30. On Benjamin as a thinker who anticipated the Shoah, see the essential work by Enzo Traverso, *L'Histoire déchirée. Auschwitz et les intellectuels* (Paris: Cerf, 1998).

31. Daniel Bensaïd has some fine pages on this in *Le Pari mélancolique* (Paris: Fayard, 1997), pp. 244–58. And there is an analysis of great finesse of Benjamin's 'melancholic Marxism' in the work of the Brazilian philosopher Leandro Konder, *Walter Benjamin, o marxismo da melancolia* (Rio de Janeiro: Editoria Campus, 1989)

32. Margaret Cohen, *Profane Illumination. Walter Benjamin and the Paris of Surrealist Revolution* (Berkeley: University of California Press, 1993), pp. 1–2.

33. See my essay 'Walter Benjamin et le surréalisme: histoire d'un enchantement révolutionnaire', *L'Étoile du Matin. Surréalisme et marxisme* (Paris: Éditions Syllepse, 2000).

34. The main texts concerned are 'Experience and Poverty' (1933), 'The Author as Producer' (1934) and, though only to a certain degree, 'The Work of Art in the Age of its Technical Reproducibility' (1935).

35. In this lecture, Benjamin brings out the 'decidedly religious' dualism between life and the *automaton* that one finds in the Gothic tales of E. T. A. Hoffmann, Oskar Panizza, Edgar Allan Poe and Alfred Kubin. The tales of the great German Romantic storyteller, inspired by the sense of a secret identity between the automatic and the satanic, perceive the life of everyday man as 'the product of a vile artificial

mechanism, governed from within by Satan'. See W. Benjamin, 'E. T. A. Hoffmann und Oskar Panizza', *GS*, II, 2, pp. 644–7.

36. W. Benjamin, *The Arcades Project*, p. 804; *Charles Baudelaire: A Lyric Poet in the Era of High Capitalism* (London: NLB, 1973), p. 135.

37. W. Benjamin, 'Johann Jakob Bachofen', *SW*, 3, pp. 11–24. Benjamin takes his inspiration from the Freudian-Marxist interpretation of Bachofen proposed by Erich Fromm.

38. Ibid., p. 12.

39. Ibid., p. 19.

40. Ibid., p. 20.

41. W. Benjamin, *Charles Baudelaire: A Lyric Poet in the Era of High Capitalism,* pp. 139, 141.

42. R. Tiedemann, 'Nachwort', in W. Benjamin, *Charles Baudelaire* (Frankfurt: Suhrkamp, 1980), pp. 205–6.

43. W. Benjamin, 'Eduard Fuchs, Collector and Historian', *SW*, 3, pp. 266–7.

44. Ibid., p. 273.

45. W. Benjamin, *The Arcades Project*, p. 460.

46. W. Benjamin, Ibid., *GS*, V, II, p. 820.

47. *Correspondence*, p. 393; Jean Selz, 'Benjamin in Ibiza', in Gary Smith (ed.), *On Walter Benjamin. Critical Essays and Recollections* (Cambridge, MA, and London: MIT Press, 1988), p. 358. On this subject, see the essay by Enzo Traverso, 'Walter Benjamin et Léon Trotsky', *Quatrième Internationale*, 37–38, 1990.

48. Letter cited by R. Tiedemann, *Dialektik im Stillstand. Versuche zum Spätwerk Walter Benjamins* (Frankfurt: Suhrkamp, 1983), p. 121.

49. Heinrich Brandler, a former leader of the KPD, expelled in 1928 and founder of the anti-Stalinist KPO (*KPD-Opposition*), was also an exile in France in 1939–40.

50. W. Benjamin, 'Note on Brecht,' *SW*, 4, p. 159. 'Blücher is right', Benjamin admits, to criticize both Brecht's poems and his own commentary.

51. Letter quoted by R. Tiedemann, *Dialektik im Stillstand. Versuche zum Spätwerk Walter Benjamins*, p. 122.

A Reading of the 'Theses "On the Concept of History"'

1. 'I have just completed a number of theses on the concept of history. These theses connect, on the one hand, with the views that are outlined in chapter 1 of the 'Fuchs'. They must, on the other, serve as theoretical armature to the second essay on Baudelaire. They represent a first attempt at pinning down an aspect of history that must establish an irremediable break [*scission*] between our way of seeing and the

survivals of positivism which, in my view, mark out so profoundly even those concepts of history which are, in themselves, closest and most familiar to us' (*GS*, I, 3, p. 1225). This last part is a transparent reference to what he will refer to in the 'Theses' as 'vulgar Marxism'.

2. Social Democratic doctrine was often neo-Kantian in inspiration, but that orientation was not necessarily in contradiction with the positivist option in the field of the social sciences, as the work of Eduard Bernstein so clearly shows.

3. Letter of April 1940 in *GS*, I, 3, pp. 1226–7.

4. Letter cited in the critical apparatus of volume I, 3 of *GS*, p. 1226.

5. '[I]n short the little treatise is clear and presents complex issues simply (despite its metaphors and its judaisms [*metaphorik und judaismen*]) and it is frightening to think how few people there are who are prepared even to misunderstand such a piece.' Bertolt Brecht, *Journals 1934–1955*, trans. by Hugh Rorrison, ed. John Willett and Ralph Manheim (New York: Routledge, 1996), p. 159.

6. Gershom Scholem and Theodor W. Adorno (eds), *The Correspondence of Walter Benjamin 1910–1940* (Chicago and London: University of Chicago Press, 1994), p. 300.

7. 'Goethe's Elective Affinities', *SW*, I, pp. 297–360. On the concept of elective affinity and its itinerary from alchemy to the sociology of Max Weber by way of Goethe, see my *Redemption and Utopia: Jewish Liberation Thought in Central Europe* (Stanford: Stanford University Press, 1998).

8. G. Scholem, *Thesen über den Begriff der Gerechtigkeit*, 1919–1925, Scholem Archive, Hebrew University of Jerusalem, p. 3.

9. In preparing the translation, the version of the 'Theses' published in W. Benjamin, *Selected Writings*, volume 4, 1938–1940, translated by Edmund Jephcott and others (Cambridge, MA, and London: The Belknap Press of the University of Harvard Press, 2003) has been used [Trans.].

10. Gianfranco Bonola, Michele Ranchetti (eds), Walter Benjamin, *Sul concetto di storia* (Turin: Einaudi, 1997),

11. W. Benjamin, *SW*, 4, pp. 401–11.

12. Edgar Allan Poe, 'Maelzel's Chess Player', 1836.

13. R. Tiedemann, *Dialektik im Stillstand*, p. 118.

14. W. Benjamin, *SW*, 3, p. 97.

15. *GS*, I, 3, p. 1235. This is passage is also included in *The Arcades Project*, p. 470 [Trans.].

16. The articles by Kaiser, Greffrath and Kittsteiner can be found in Peter Bulthaup, *Materialien zu Benjamins Thesen 'Über den Begriff der Geschichte'* (Frankfurt: Suhrkamp, 1975).

17. On this question, see my book *The War of Gods: Religion and Politics in Latin America* (London: Verso, 1996).

18. The term *Erlösung*, which Benjamin very probably took from Franz Rosenzweig's book *Der Stern der Erlösung* (The Star of Redemption), has a signification that is both – and inseparably – theological and political, referring both to salvation and to deliverance or liberation. The same is true also of the equivalent Hebrew term *ge'ulah*.

19. *The Arcades Project*, p. 479.

20. *GS* I, 3, p. 1225.

21. *The Arcades Project*, pp. 478–9.

22. M. Horkheimer, *Kritische Theorie* (Frankfurt: S. Fischer, 1968), I, pp. 198–9.

23. *The Arcades Project*, p. 471 Translation modified.

24. Ibid. Translation modified. Gérard Raulet is one of the very few writers to take account of Lotze's writings in deciphering thesis II. His interpretation is interesting, but suffers from a dualistic view of Benjamin's thought which attributes to him, as an ultimate assumption, 'a change of axis: the radical substitution of messianic for secular time.' See G. Raulet, *Le Caractère destructeur. Esthétique, théologie et politique chez Walter Benjamin* (Paris: Aubier, 1997), p. 207. In our view, there is not a substitution, but a *correspondence* between the two axes. We shall return to this point.

25. Heinrich Regius (Max Horkheimer), *Dämmerung. Notizen in Deutschland* (Zurich: Verlag Opnecht und Helbling, 1924), pp. 272.

26. We shall come back to this cabbalistic term in the commentary on Thesis III.

27. According to Buber, for Hassidism God does not wish for redemption without the participation of human beings: the human generations have been granted a 'cooperative force' (*mitwirkende Kraft*), an active messianic force (*messianische Kraft*). See *Die chassidische Bücher* (Berlin: Schocken, 1927), pp. xxiii, xxvi, xxvii.

28. See R. Tiedemann, *Studien zur Philosophie Walter Benjamins* (Frankfurt: Suhrkamp, 1973), p. 138.

29. This is the King James version. Richmond Lattimore renders this passage as 'for when I am weak, then I am strong'. *Acts and Letters of the Apostles* (New York: Farrar Straus Giroux, 1982), p. 153 [Trans.].

30. G. Agamben, *Le Temps qui reste. Un commentaire de l''Épitre aux Romains'* (Paris: Payot, 2000), pp. 218–19. It is true that this Christian *kerygma* has a Jewish origin in the Old Testament figure of the Messiah as 'suffering servant of the Lord'.

31. J. Habermas, 'L'actualité de W. Benjamin', *Revue d'esthétique*, 1, p. 112.

32. I am drawing here on the fine text by J–M. Gagnebin, *Histoire et narration chez W. Benjamin*, p. 157. Cf. Benjamin, 'Paralipomena to "On the Concept of History": Should criticism and prophecy be the categories that come together in the "redemption" [*Rettung*] of the past?' (*SW*, 4, p. 407).

33. T. Adorno, 'Progress', *Critical Models. Interventions and Catchwords* (New York: Columbia University Press, 1998), p. 145.

34. W. Benjamin, 'Paralipomena', *SW*, 4, p. 404.

35. I. Wohlfarth, 'On the messianic structure of Walter Benjamin's last reflections', *Glyph*, 3 (Baltimore: Johns Hopkins University Press, 1978), p. 152.

36. W. Benjamin, 'The Storyteller. Observations on the Works of Nikolai Leskov', *SW*, 3, p. 158.

37. H. Lotze, *Mikrokosmus. Ideen zur Naturgeschichte und Geschichte der Menschheit. Versuch einer Anthropologie* (Leipzig: Verlag von S. Hirzel, 1864), vol. 3, pp. 51–2, 56.

38. According to Scholem, in cabbalistic language *tikkun* designates the restoration or re-establishment of the cosmic order laid down by divine providence, thanks to messianic redemption; the collapse of the force of evil and the *catastrophic end of the historic order*, which are *simply the obverse of redemption*. Adam's original sin can be abolished only by the coming of the Messianic Kingdom, thanks to which things will return to their original places: *Ha-Shavat Kol ha-Devarim le-Havaiatam* – the Christian equivalent of which would be the concept of *apokatastasis* (*Encyclopaedia Judaica*, vol. 9, 1932, pp. 659–63, 697–8, 703).

39. *Correspondence*, p. 401.

40. 'Certain elements creep into such a restoratively oriented utopianism . . . which derive from the vision of a completely new state of the Messianic world. The completely new order has elements of the completely old, but even this old order does not consist of the actual past; rather, it is a past transformed and transfigured in a dream brightened by the rays of utopianism.' Scholem, *The Messianic Idea in Judaism* (London: Allen & Unwin, 1971), p. 4.

   Where Benjamin is concerned, J–M. Gagnebin rightly observes that the theme of *restitutio* or *apokatastasis* is not a mere restorative project: it is indeed a recovery of the past, but 'at the same time – and because the past, as past, can only return in a non-identity to itself – an opening onto the future, a constitutive incompletion'. *Histoire et narration chez Walter Benjamin* (Paris: L'Harmattan, 1994), p. 26.

41. *The Arcades Project*, p. 698.

42. F. Engels, *The Peasant War in Germany* (Moscow: Progress Publishers, 1956), p. 56.

43. The reference is to the translation into French of the 'Theses' made by Benjamin himself and included in the *Gesammelte Schriften*, I, pp. 1260–6. The term *Zuversicht*, which Benjamin translates as *foi*, is rendered here, more conventionally, as 'confidence' [Trans.].

44. Letter to G. Scholem, 16 September 1924, *Correspondence*, p. 248.

45. K. Marx and F. Engels, 'Manifesto of the Communist Party', in D. Fernbach (ed.), *The Revolutions of 1848. Political Writings – Volume 1* (Harmondsworth: Penguin in association with *New Left Review*, 1973), p. 68.

46. Curiously, in the Paralipomena, Benjamin seems to reject the possibility that the peasant war may serve as a reference for modern workers' struggles. He is not referring to Engels or Bloch, but to the work of the historian Zimmermann (GS, I, 3, p. 1236; this passage is not included in SW, 4 [Trans.]). This remark was not, however, incorporated into the 'Theses'. Might he have changed his mind?

47. Plekhanov argues that the victory of the socialist programme is as inevitable as the rising of the sun tomorrow . . .

48. GS, I, 3, p. 1248.

49. In 'Two Tactics of Social-Democracy in the Democratic Revolution' (1905), Lenin observes that the Commune was a workers' government 'that was unable to, and could not, at that time distinguish between the elements of a democratic revolution and a socialist revolution, a government that confused the tasks of fighting for a republic with those of fighting for socialism . . . In short . . . it was a government *such as ours should not be.*' V. I. Lenin, *Selected Works* (London: Lawrence & Wishart, 1969), pp. 101–2. The expression *'ours'* refers to the future democratic Russian government Lenin was calling for.

50. J.-M. Gagnebin, 'W. Benjamin o a historia aberta'. Preface to W. Benjamin, *Obras Escolhidas*, I (São Paulo: Brasiliense, 1985), p. 16.

51. Cf. K. Greffrath, 'Der historische Materialist als dialektischer Historiker', in P. Bulthaupt (ed.), *Materialien zu Benjamins Thesen*, p. 226.

52. GS, I, 3, p. 1242.

53. GS, I, 3, p. 1263.

54. W. Benjamin, 'Notes sur les Tableaux parisiens de Baudelaire' (1939), GS, I, 2, p. 748.

55. R. Tiedemann, 'Historischer Materialismus oder politischer Messianismus? Politische Gehalt in der Geschichtsphilosophie Walter Benjamins', in P. Bulthaupt (ed.), *Materialien zu Benjamins Thesen*, pp. 93–4.

56. W. Benjamin, 'A Chronicle of Germany's Unemployed', SW, 4, p. 130.

57. Cf. Chrissoula Kambas, 'Wider den "Geist der Zeit". Die antifaschistische Politik Fritz Leibs und Walter Benjamin', in J. Taubes (ed.), *Der Fürst dieser Welt* (Munich: Carl Schmitt und die Folgen, 1983), pp. 582–3. Lieb and Benjamin shared the conviction that Fascism had to be resisted by force of arms.

58. Numa Denis Fustel de Coulanges (1830–99) was a declared opponent of democracy and the Republic. As a defender of the family, religion and property, Fustel rejected universal suffrage, which he saw as being responsible for the Empire, the defeat of 1870 and the Commune. As a positivist, he argued that 'history is pure science, a science like physics or geology'. See C. Delacroix, F. Dosse and P. Garcia, *Les Courants historiques en France, XIXe et XXe siècles* (Paris: Armand Colin, 1999), pp. 73–6 and F. Hartog, *Le XIXe siècle et l'histoire. Le cas Fustel de Coulanges* (Paris: PUF, 1988), pp. 341–2.

59. W. Benjamin, *The Origin of German Tragic Drama*, trans. John Osborne (London: Verso, 1998).

60. V. Cousin, *Cours de philosophie. Introduction à la philosophie de l'histoire*, 1828 (Paris: Fayard, 1991), p. 242, quoted by Michèle Riot-Sarcey, *Le Réel et l'utopie. Essai sur le politique du XIXe siècle* (Paris: Albin Michel, 1998), p. 44.

61. Friedrich Nietzsche, *On the Advantage and Disadvantage of History for Life*, trans. Peter Preuss (Indianapolis: Hackett, 1980), pp. 47, 49, 52.

62. Like Brecht in his novel *Die Geschäfte des Herrn Julius Caesar* or in his play *The Trial of Lucullus*, Benjamin was interested in the parallels between Roman and modern imperialism. Brecht thought – probably wrongly – that Benjamin's theses had been influenced by the reading of his Caesar novel. See B. Brecht, *Arbeitsjournal*, vol. 1, 1938–42, ed. Werner Hecht (Frankfurt: Suhrkamp, 1973), p. 294.

63. In *The Arcades Project*, we find several references to the book by Ferdinand Noack, *Triumph und Triumphbogen*, published in 1928 by the Warburg Library of Leipzig (pp. 96–7), to Victor Hugo's poems on the Arc de Triomphe (pp. 93–5), together with a quotation from Arsène Houssaye describing Napoleon III entering Paris 'beneath two thousand triumphal arches' (p. 138).

64. W. Benjamin, 'Berlin Childhood Around 1900', *SW*, 3, p. 349. An interesting example not cited by Benjamin, but which he doubtless knew, is the Marktbrunnen (Market Fountain) in Mainz: this magnificent Renaissance masterpiece was erected by Archbishop Albrecht of Brandenburg to commemorate the triumph of the princes over the peasant revolt of 1525. The words *Conspiratio rusticorum prostrata* are carved on this monument, which thus directly refers to the victory of the powerful in the class struggle.

65. Bertolt Brecht, *Poems 1913–1956*, trans. Michael Hamburger (London and New York: Methuen, 1976).

66. *GS*, I, 3, p. 1240. Cf. Irving Wohlfarth, 'Smashing the Kaleidoscope: Walter Benjamin's Critique of Cultural History' and my own essay, 'Against the Grain: The Dialectical Conception of Culture in Walter Benjamin's Theses of 1940', both of which are published in Michael Steinberg (ed.), *Walter Benjamin and the Demands of History* (Ithaca: Cornell University Press, 1996).

67. Richard Wolin, *Walter Benjamin. An Aesthetic of Redemption* (New York: Columbia University Press, 1982), pp. 263–4. This is, in my view, one of the best books on the whole of Benjamin's work.

68. The anti-bourgeois component of nineteenth-century culture is well brought out by Dolf Oehler in his markedly Benjaminian, *Ein Höllensturz der Alten Welt. Zur Selbstforschung der Moderne nach dem Juni 1848* (Frankfurt: Suhrkamp, 1988). See also, by the same author, *Pariser Bilder I (1830–1848). Antibourgeoise Ästhetik bei Baudelaire, Daumier und Heine* (Frankfurt: Suhrkamp, 1979).

69. We find the political equivalent of that work of art in the writings of the Indigenist Peruvian socialist José Carlos Mariátegui during the years 1927–30, particularly the *Seven Interpretive Essays on Peruvian Reality* (Austin: University of Texas Press, 1971).

70. E. Galeano, 'El tigre azul y nuestra tierra prometida', *Nosotros decimos no* (Mexico City: Siglo XXI, 1991).

71. *The Origin of German Tragic Drama* (London: Verso, 1998), pp. 65, 59. In December 1930, Benjamin had sent his book to Carl Schmitt, accompanied by a letter expressing his admiration (*Hochschätzung*) and acknowledging the influence of his works on the *Trauerspielbuch* (*GS*, I, 3, p. 887).

72. 'The superiority that it [Fascism] has over the Left is expressed in the – not inconsiderable – fact that the Left opposes it in the name of the historical norm, of a kind of average historical constitution' (*GS*, I, 3, p. 1246).

73. *GS*, I, 3, p. 1244.

74. One may take the view, with Rainer Rochlitz – whose book contains some interesting insights, particularly where Benjamin's aesthetic ideas are concerned – that this objective is utopian and unrealistic, and criticize the author of the theses for his stubborn refusal to trust in 'gradual change', in the inevitable 'compromises and half-measures' of Social Democracy. But to attribute to him in Thesis VIII 'the recourse to an authoritarian politics indissociable from the "state of exception" coined by Carl Schmitt' is to misunderstand him. See R. Rochlitz, *Le Désenchantement de l'art. La philosophie de Walter Benjamin* (Paris: Gallimard, 1992, p. 271). Benjamin aspires precisely, for all he is worth, to the *true* exception, which is the end of authoritarian powers, and this is as far removed as can be from all the 'states of exception' in Carl Schmitt's sense.

75. W. Benjamin, 'Conversation above the Corso', *SW*, 3, p. 26.

76. *The Origin of German Tragic Drama*, p. 166.

77. Max Horkheimer and Theodor W. Adorno, *Dialectic of Enlightenment*, trans. John Cumming (London: Allen Lane, 1973), p. 161.

78. *SW*, 3, p. 12.

79. *SW*, 3, p. 34.

80. 'Central Park', *SW*, 4, pp. 184–5

81. *The Arcades Project*, pp. 106, 15.

82. F. Schiller, 'The Nature and Value of Universal History: An Inaugural Lecture [1789]', *History and Theory*, vol. 11, 3, 1972, p. 333.

83. G. W. F. Hegel, *Elements of the Philosophy of Right* (Cambridge: Cambridge Unversity Press, 1991), p. 371.

84. G. W. F. Hegel, *Lectures on the Philosophy of World History. Introduction: Reason in History*, trans. by H. B. Nisbet (Cambridge: Cambridge University Press, 1975), pp. 68–9.

85. Ibid., p. 32.
86. G. Scholem, *Walter Benjamin. Die Geschichte einer Freundschaft* (Frankfurt: Suhrkamp, 1975), p. 252. The expression 'after the Jewish fashion' is to be found in Benjamin's dedication of the book to his sister Dora. Let us remember also that writers close to fascism, such as Ernst Jünger – the subject of a radical critique by Benjamin in 1930 – had described war as a 'storm of steel' (*Stahlgewitter* was the title of one of his first books, published in 1920)
87. 'Paralipomena to "On the Concept of History"', *SW*, 4, p. 401.
88. *SW*, 4, p. 402.
89. G. Scholem, 'Walter Benjamin and his Angel', in Gary Smith (ed.), *On Walter Benjamin*, p. 84.
90. *SW*, 4, p. 403.
91. Scholem, 'Walter Benjamin and his Angel', p. 83; Benjamin, *SW*, 4, pp. 405–6. As Irving Wohlfarth observes in his remarkable essay on messianism in Benjamin's last texts, we have here a dialectical 'spiral' rather than a circle, because the messianic future is the *Aufhebung* – in the Hegelian sense – of the whole of past history. See I. Wohlfarth, 'On the Messianic Structure of Walter Benjamin's Last Reflexions', p. 186.
92. As an example of what Benjamin felt to be a betrayal of the anti-Fascist struggle, we may cite the resolution adopted in July 1939 by the Central Committee of the KPD which, while reaffirming its opposition to Hitler, 'hail[ed] the non-aggression pact between the Soviet Union and Germany' and called for 'the development of economic relations with the USSR in a spirit of sincere and unreserved friendship between the two countries'! See Theo Pirker (ed.), *Utopie und Mythos der Weltrevolution. Zur Geschichte der Komintern* 1920–1940 (Munich: Deutscher Taschenbuch Verlag, 1964), p. 286.
93. See Irving Wohlfarth, '"Männer aus der Fremde": Walter Benjamin and the "German–Jewish Parnassus"', *New German Critique*, 70, winter 1997, p. 55. Somma Morgenstern refers in a (late, 1972) letter to G. Scholem to conversations with Benjamin shortly after the signing of the pact in 1939. See Hans Puttnies, Gary Smith, *Benjaminiana* (Giessen: Anabas, 1991), pp. 196–7.
94. Not to speak of Leon Trotsky who had, from his exile in Mexico, denounced the pact as a positive 'betrayal' that had made Stalin 'Hitler's new friend' and his 'quartermaster'. See Trotsky's articles of 2–4 September in *Writings of Leon Trotsky* 1939–40 (New York: Pathfinder Press, 1973).
95. Friedrich Nietzsche, *On the Advantage and Disadvantage of History for Life*, p. 49. The German text reads: 'Er schwimmt immer gegen die geschichtlichen Wellen . . . während die Lüge rings um ihn herum ihre glitzernden Netze spinnt.'
96. *GS*, I, 3, p. 1232. This section is not translated in the 'Paralipomena' in *SW*, vol. 4.

97. *GS*, I, 3, p. 1264.

98. M. Horkheimer, 'The Authoritarian State' in: A. Arato and E. Gebhardt (eds), *The Essential Frankfurt School Reader* (New York: Urizen Books, 1978), pp. 106–7.

99. W. Benjamin, 'Eduard Fuchs, Collector and Historian', *SW*, 3, p. 274. Cf. p. 266: Positivism overlooked the fact that the development of technology 'was decisively conditioned by capitalism'. And the positivists among the Social Democratic theorists 'misunderstood the destructive side of this development because they were alienated from the destructive side of dialectics'. The destructive potential shows itself primarily in military technology: Benjamin stressed – in *One-Way Street*, for example – bombing, chemical warfare and poison gas, but even he, the most pessimistic of all thinkers, could not foresee what the modern barbarism of the Second World War would be like.

100. Benjamin is perhaps referring to an article by Marx dating from 1847 which comments on some of the most sinister developments of capitalism, such as the Poor Laws or the workhouses – 'these Bastilles of the workers' – in the following terms: 'Barbarism reappears, but created in the lap of civilization itself and belonging to it; hence leprous barbarism, barbarism as leprosy of civilization' (K. Marx, 'Wages', *Marx–Engels Collected Works*, vol. 6).

101. E. Ferri, *Socialism and Positive Science (Darwin – Spencer – Marx)*, trans. Edith C. Harvey (London: Independent Labour Party, 1909), pp. 114–15.

102. The German workers' party 'is working its way to the fore as certainly and inexorably as once Christianity – so certainly that the rate at which its velocity will increase, and hence the actual time of its ultimate victory, already permits of mathematical calculation' ('Engels to Karl Kautsky in Zurich, London 8 November 1884', *Marx–Engels Collected Works*, vol. 47, p. 213). See the insightful commentary on positivism and evolutionism in certain of the writings of Marx and Engels in Étienne Balibar, *La Crainte des masses. Dialectique et philosophie avant et après Marx* (Paris: Galilée, 1997), pp. 273–5. The question remains of why Benjamin does not refer – or refers only little – to Marx and Engels in his critical remarks: I shall return to this point in the conclusion.

103. *GS*, I, 3, p. 1249.

104. Benjamin's intuitions regarding Fascist technocracy are confirmed by recent historical research. See, for example, Jeffrey Herf, *Reactionary Modernism: Technology, Culture and Politics in Weimar and the Third Reich* (Cambridge: Cambridge University Press, 1986); Zygmunt Bauman, *Modernity and the Holocaust* (Cambridge: Polity Press, 1989); Enzo Traverso, *Understanding the Nazi Genocide. Marxism after Auschwitz* (London: Pluto Press, 1999). Herf characterizes the ideology of the Third Reich as 'reactionary modernism' and within this framework examines the writings of well-known Fascist ideologues and the documents of associations of pro-Nazi engineers. As for the

sociologist Zygmunt Bauman, he analyses the genocide of the Jews and the Gypsies as a typical product of rational bureaucratic culture and as one of the possible outcomes of the civilizing process, as rationalization and centralization of violence, and as social production of moral indifference. 'Like everything else done in the modern – rational, planned, scientifically informed, expert, efficiently managed, coordinated – way, the Holocaust left behind . . . all its alleged pre-modern equivalents, exposing them as primitive, wasteful and ineffective by comparison' (p. 89). Lastly, according to Enzo Traverso, we find in the Nazi death camps a combination of different institutions typical of modernity: the prison described by Foucault, the capitalist factory of which Marx wrote, Taylor's 'scientific organization of work' and 'rational-bureaucratic administration' according to Max Weber.

105. J. Habermas, 'Walter Benjamin: Consciousness-Raising or Rescuing Critique', in Gary Smith (ed.), *On Walter Benjamin*, pp. 113–4.

106. According to Weber, ' "Domination" (*Herrschaft*) is the probability that a command with a specific given content will be obeyed by a given group of persons', *Economy and Society*, vol. I (Berkeley, Los Angeles and London: University of California Press, 1978), p. 53.

107. In 'Paris, the Capital of the Nineteenth Century', he writes: 'Marx took a stand against Carl Grün in order to defend Fourier and to accentuate his "colossal conception of man." He considered Fourier the only man besides Hegel to have revealed the essential mediocrity of the petty bourgeois . . . One of the most remarkable features of the Fourierist utopia is that it never advocated the exploitation of nature by man, an idea that became widespread in the following period' (*The Arcades Project*, p. 17). As Philippe Ivernet pertinently observed, Benjamin 'crossed' Marx's thinking with that of Fourier, 'in such a way that they corrected and straightened each other out and lent each other a reciprocal dynamism', 'Paris capitale du Front populaire ou la vie posthume du XIXe siècle', in H. Wismann (ed.), *Walter Benjamin et Paris* (Paris, Éditions du Cerf, 1986), p. 266.

108. *The Arcades Project*, p. 361.

109. Fourier's machinery of the passions 'produces the land of milk and honey, the primeval wish symbol that Fourier's utopia has filled with new life' (*The Arcades Project*, p. 5). Cf. p. 361, where Benjamin moves directly from Fourier to Bachofen. See also the 1935 article on Bachofen which I referred to above.

110. F. Nietzsche, *On the Advantage and Disadvantage of History for Life*, pp. 7–8 (translation modified).

111. Some passages from Lukács's book will show clearly that it constitutes the main theoretical reference for Thesis XII: 'the knowledge of reality provided by the dialectical method is likewise inseparable from the class standpoint of the proletariat'. 'In the case of the class struggle of the proletariat, the war for the liberation of the last

oppressed class, the revelation of the unvarnished truth became both a war-cry and the most potent weapon.' G. Lukács, *History and Class Consciousness* (London: The Merlin Press, 1971), pp. 21, 224.

112. W. Benjamin, 'Conversations with Brecht', in *Aesthetics and Politics* (London: New Left Books, 1977), p. 98.

113. F. Nietzsche, *On the Genealogy of Morals*, trans. Douglas Smith (Oxford: Oxford University Press, 1996), pp. 22, 35. It is important to observe that hatred and vengeance – 'the intoxication of sweet revenge ("sweeter than honey", as Homer described it . . .)' (ibid., p. 32) – are not condemned by Nietzsche, provided that they are directed against a personal enemy – Achilles fighting Hector to avenge his friend Patroclus – and not against 'injustice'. For Benjamin, precisely the opposite is the case.

114. G. Geffroy, *L'Enfermé* (Paris: Les Éditions G. Crès, 1926), vol. II, pp. 19–20. Miguel Abensour argues that 'the shadow of Blanqui runs through' Benjamin's Theses. 'As though the author had woven into his theses an esoteric commentary on Blanqui's manuscripts. One recognizes in them the leap of the tiger. As a practitioner of collage, Benjamin acts as though he is diverting the weapons forged by Blanqui against positivism in order to strike his own blows against those who pour out their hearts in the brothel of historicism.' M. Abensour, 'Libérer l'enfermé', postface to A. Blanqui, *Instruction pour une prise d'armes* (Paris: La Tête des Feuilles, 1972), p. 206. See also M. Abensour, 'Walter Benjamin entre mélancolie et révolution. Passages Blanqui', in Heinz Wismann (ed.), *Walter Benjamin et Paris* (Paris: Éditions du Cerf, 1986).

115. W. Benjamin, 'Central Park', SW 4, p. 188. In his fine book on Benjamin, Daniel Bensaïd notes that he shared with Blanqui a particular melancholy conception of history, based on the hellish vision of the eternal return of defeat. See D. Bensaïd, *Walter Benjamin. Sentinelle messianique* (Paris, Plon, 1980), p. 43.

116. *GS*, I, 3, p. 1264.

117. Quoted by Chryssoula Kambas in *Walter Benjamin im Exil. Zum Verhältnis von Literaturpolitik und Ästhetik* (Tübingen: Max Niemeyer, 1983), p. 218.

118. *GS*, I, 3, p. 1240.

119. *The Arcades Project*, p. 667 (translation modified). The German original here is: 'Die Erfahrung unserer Generation: dass der Kapitalismus keines natürlichen Todes sterben wird' (*GS*, V, 2, p. 819).

120. A preparatory note reveals a programme for a general critique of theories of progress, Marx's theory included: 'Critique of the theory of progress in Marx. Progress is defined here by the development of the productive forces. But to these belongs the human being and hence the proletariat. Consequently, the question of criteria is merely displaced' (*GS*, I, 3, p. 1239). Unfortunately, Benjamin was not able to

develop this critique of a concept – that of 'productive forces' – which occupies a central place in all the productivist, economistic, evolutionary variants of the Marxist theory of progress.

121. Letter of 12 June 1941, in W. Benjamin, *GS*, VII, 2 (*Nachträge*), p. 774. It should be noted that, according to Adorno, 'no other work of Benjamin's is so close to our intentions'.

122. Cf. Ralf Konersmann, *Erstarrte Unruhe. Walter Benjamins Begriff der Geschichte* (Frankfurt: Fischer, 1991), pp. 44–5.

123. W. Benjamin, 'Karl Kraus', *SW*, 2, p. 451.

124. W. Benjamin, *The Arcades Project*, pp. 66, 71–2, 73.

125. *GS*, I, 3, p. 1249

126. K. Marx, 'The Eighteenth Brumaire of Louis Bonaparte', *Surveys from Exile. Political Writings, Volume* 2 (London: Penguin Books in association with *New Left Review*, 1977), pp. 143–249.

127. *GS*, I, 3, p. 1246.

128. *GS*, I, 3, p. 1236.

129. W. Benjamin, 'Eduard Fuchs, Collector and Historian', *SW*, 3, p. 269.

130. *Thomas Münzer als Theologe der Revolution* (Frankfurt: Suhrkamp, 1985).

131. *GS*, I, 3, p. 1242.

132. *GS*, I, 3, p. 1265.

133. Referring to Jewish rituals, and in particular to the Passover Haggadah, Yosef Hayim Yerushalmi writes: 'Memory here is no longer recollection, which still preserves a sense of distance, but reactualization'. *Zakhor. Jewish History and Jewish Memory* (Seattle and London: University of Washington Press, 1996), p. 44.

134. See E. P. Thompson, 'Time, Work-Discipline and Industrial Capitalism', in *Customs in Common* (London: Penguin Books, 1991).

135. W. Benjamin, 'Trauerspiel and Tragedy', *SW*, I, pp. 55–8; 'The Concept of Criticism in German Romanticism', *SW*, I, pp. 116–200.

136. S. Mowinckel, *He that Cometh* (Oxford: Basil Blackwell, 1956), p. 106.

137. W. Benjamin, 'Central Park', *SW*, 4, p. 170.

138. W. Benjamin, 'Eduard Fuchs', *SW*, 3, p. 262.

139. Ibid.

140. A passage from a communiqué of 14 February 1994 from the Clandestine Revolutionary Indigenous Committee of the EZLN makes the point: 'The words of the oldest of our elders also brought hope for our history. And in their words the image of one like us appeared: Emiliano Zapata. And in that image we saw the place where our paths should lead to be true. And it returned our history of struggle to our blood, and our hands filled with the cries of our people, and dignity returned, once again, to our mouths, and our eyes saw a new world.' Sub-commandante Marcos, *Ya basta!*

Les insurgés zapatistes racontent un an de révolte au Chiapas (Paris: Éditions Dagorno, 1994), p. 166.

141. The Mexican Revolution, the first great social revolution of the century, overthrew the dictatorship of General Porfirio Díaz in 1911. The peasant armies, led in the South by Emiliano Zapata and in the North by Francisco Villa, took the capital, Mexico City, in 1914, but were unable to create a revolutionary government or impose their radical agrarian programme. The moderate politicians and generals who took over the leadership of the revolution succeeded – after first defeating Zapata and Villa and having them assassinated – in imposing their lasting hegemony on the country. Presenting themselves as heirs to the ideals of the revolution of 1911–17 – after the radical interlude of Lázaro Cárdenas's government – they founded the Partido Revolucionario Institucional or Institutional Revolutionary Party in the 1940s and it remained in power until the end of the twentieth century.

142. As S. Mosès so aptly observes, 'What Benjamin . . . borrows from religious experience is precisely the extreme attention to the qualitative difference of time, to the matchless uniqueness of each moment. If there is a point at which political vigilance connects most intimately to religious sensibility it is certainly here – at the very nub of the perception of time' (*L'Ange de l'histoire*, p. 166).

143. Cf. the letter to Scholem of 15 September 1919: 'I have again read some things by Péguy. In this instance, I feel that I am being addressed by an unbelievably kindred spirit. Might I be permitted to say that *nothing* written has ever impressed me so very much because of how close it is to me, because of my feeling of oneness with it . . . Immense melancholy that has been mastered.' G. Scholem and T. W. Adorno (eds), *The Correspondence of Walter Benjamin,* trans. Manfred R. Jacobson and Evelyn M. Jacobson (Chicago and London: The University of Chicago Press, 1994), p. 147.

144. C. Péguy, 'Clio. Dialogue de l'histoire et de l'âme payenne' (1909–1912), *Œuvres en prose* (Paris: La Pléiade, 1968), vol. I, pp. 127–31, 180–81, 286, 299–300. See also the article by Helga Tiedemann-Bartels, 'La mémoire est toujours de guerre. Benjamin et Péguy', in H. Wismann (ed.), *Walter Benjamin et Paris* (Paris: Éditions du Cerf, 1986), pp. 133–43, and D. Bensaïd, *Moi la Révolution* (Paris: Gallimard, 1989).

145. In a first version of this thesis to be found in *The Arcades Project*, in place of the concept of monad there appears that of the 'dialectical image'. See *The Arcades Project*, p. 475 (N 10a, 3).

146. Commenting on this passage on the 'messianic arrest of happening', Herbert Marcuse wrote in 1964: 'Rarely was the truth of critical theory expressed in such exemplary form: the revolutionary struggle demands the halting of what is happening and what has happened. Before it can give itself some sort of positive goal, this negation is the first positive act. What the human being has done to other humans and to nature must stop and stop radically – only afterwards can freedom and justice

begin.' H. Marcuse, 'Revolution und Kritik der Gewalt. Zur Geschichtsphilosophie Walter Benjamins', in P. Bulthaupt, *Materialien zu Benjamins Thesen*, pp. 25–6.

147. *GS*, I, 3, p. 1243.

148. This is how Scholem interprets the Marxist metamorphosis of Jewish messianism: 'The difference between the modern "theory of revolution" . . . and the messianic idea of Judaism consists, in large measure, in a transposition of terms. In its new form, history becomes a prehistory . . . This is the attitude underlying the writings of the most important ideologues of revolutionary messianism, such as Ernst Bloch, Walter Benjamin, Theodor Adorno and Herbert Marcuse.' *Fidélité et utopie. Essais sur le judaïsme contemporain* (Paris: Calmann-Lévy, 1978), pp. 255–6. I. Wohlfarth also observes that, in Benjamin's secularized messianism, the end of time is not the end of all history, as in orthodox messianism, but the end of what Marx would term 'prehistory'. See I. Wohlfarth, 'The Measure of the Possible', in L. Marcus and L. Nead (eds), *The Actuality of W. Benjamin* (London: Lawrence & Wishart, 1998), p. 36. These interpretations are interesting, but let us remind the reader that Benjamin does not use the term 'end of prehistory'.

149. 'Paralipomena to "On the Concept of History"', *SW*, 4, p. 404.

150. Ibid., p. 407. See also *GS*, I, 3, p. 1239.

151. Letter cited in *GS*, I, 3, p. 1226.

152. Carl Schmitt, *Political Theology. Four Chapters on the Concept of Sovereignty*, trans. George Schwab (Cambridge, MA, and London: The MIT Press, 1985), p. 36.

153. Jacob Taubes, *Die politische Theologie des Paulus* (Munich: Wilhelm Fink 1993), pp. 89–92.

154. This passage comes from one of Scholem's unpublished notebooks, entitled *Tagebuchaufzeichnungen* 1. August 1918 – 1. August 1919, Adelboden-Bern, 89 pp. This material, which is in the Scholem Archive of the Hebrew University of Jerusalem library will be published shortly by the Jüdischer Verlag (in association with Suhrkamp) of Frankfurt. I thank the editors of Scholem's manuscripts – Karlfried Gründer, Friedrich Niewöhner and Herbert Kopp-Osterbrink – for their kind authorization to publish extracts from these unpublished papers.

155. As Philippe Ivernel so aptly observes, 'in the Theses, the class struggle and Jewish messianism, far from neutralizing each other, mutually activate – or, rather, reactivate – one another, and together lead the charge against alleged historical necessity'. 'Paris, capitale du Front populaire ou la vie posthume du XIXe siècle', in Heinz Wismann, *Walter Benjamin et Paris,* p. 271.

156. W. Benjamin, 'Paralipomena' *SW*, 4, p. 407.

157. Henri Focillon, *The Life of Forms in Art*, (New York: Zone Books, 1992) p. 55.

158. *GS*, I, 3, p. 1234.

159. *The Arcades Project*, p. 461.

160. G. Agamben, *Le Temps qui reste*, p. 224. I have taken the text of this epistle from the Authorized Version. Richmond Lattimore renders the passage as follows: 'that everything in heaven and on earth should be summed up in the Christ' (*Acts and Letters of the Apostles*, p. 166) [Trans.].

161. Unlike Agamben, I do not think that *Jetztzeit* refers directly to the expression *ho nun kairos* which Paul uses in the New Testament to refer to messianic time, particularly as the term *Jetztzeit* does not appear in Luther's translation (which has: *in dieser Zeit*). Some of Agamben's suggestions are very interesting, but he tends to over-systematize: his attempt to identify Paul as the 'theologian hidden between the lines of [Benjamin's] text' – the one ensuring the automaton's victory in Thesis I – seems unconvincing to me (ibid., p. 215). Though Christian references are by no means absent from the 'Theses' – beginning with the figure of the Antichrist – it seems to me difficult to deny that the theology to which Benjamin principally makes reference is Jewish messianism.

162. On this question, see the illuminating interpretation by Françoise Proust: the messianic intervention arises 'against all expectation and in untimely fashion, and flashing up the possibility of fulfilling desires that history had buried beneath the rubble'. The messianic moment is 'that suspended moment or that suspension of time at which there emerges the fervent, incandescent, happy possibility that justice will at last come'. F. Proust, *L'Histoire à contretemps*, p. 178.

163. See I. Wohlfarth, 'The Messianic Structure', pp. 157, 171, 180.

164. G. Scholem, *Über Metaphysik, Logik und einige nicht dazu gehörende Gebiete phänomenologischer Besinnung. Mir gewidmet.* 5, Oktober 1917–30. Dezember 1917, unpublished (61 pp.), p. 27

165. I am here summarizing ideas advanced by S. Mosès, *L'Ange de l'histoire*, pp. 23–4, 195–6.

166. It seems to me that Françoise Proust is mistaken when she writes that for Benjamin 'the soothsayer is not a sorcerer . . . He does not make the future or the past appear, but rather releases them from a spell. He calls them up to disenchant them . . .' (*L'Histoire à contretemps*, p. 155)

167. See Y. H. Yerushalmi, *Zakhor*, p. 25: 'Only in Israel, and nowhere else is the injunction to remember felt as a religious imperative for an entire people. Its reverberations are everywhere, but they reach a crescendo in the Deuteronomic history and in the Prophets: "Remember the days of old, consider the years of ages past" (Deut. 32: 7) . . . "Remember what Amalek did to you . . ." (Deut. 25: 17); "O My people, remember now what Balak king of Moab plotted against you . . ." (Micah 6: 5) and, with a hammering insistence, "Remember that you were a slave in Egypt".'

168. Ibid., p. 96.

169. H. Focillon, *The Life of Formsóin Art*, p. 155; quoted in Benjamin, *GS*, I, 3, pp. 1229–30.

170. What are involved here are forms of 'messianic activism . . . lead[ing] to direct action on the historical plane' in order to 'hasten the end' of time. See Y. H. Yerushalmi, *Zakhor*, p. 24.

171. F. Rosenzweig, *Star of Redemption*, trans. William W. Hallo (London: Routledge & Kegan Paul, 1971), pp. 226–7.

172. R. Tiedemann, *Dialektik im Stillstand*, p. 130.

The Opening-up of History

1. Marx, Engels, 'Manifesto of the Communist Party', in D. Fernbach (ed.), *The Revolutions of 1848* (Harmondsworth: Penguin Books in association with *New Left Review*, 1973), p. 79.

2. Marx writes: 'Capitalist production begets, with the inexorability of a natural process, its own negation'. *Capital*, Volume One (Harmondsworth: Penguin Books in association with *New Left Review*, 1976), p. 929. The original German text is: 'Die kapitalistische Produktion erzeugt mit der Notwendigkeit eines Naturprozesses ihre eigene Negation', *Werke*, 23 (Berlin: Dietz, 1968), p. 791. In the Preface to *Capital*, Marx defines the aim of his work as the discovery of the 'law of motion of modern society' that determines 'the natural phases of its development' (ibid., p. 92).

3. See the analyses by D. Bensaïd in *Marx, l'intempestif. Grandeurs et misères d'une aventure critique* (Paris: Fayard, 1995), pp. 10, 44.

4. W. Benjamin, 'Paralipomena', *SW*, 4, p. 402.

5. This is what a great nineteenth-century revolutionary admired by Benjamin wrote in this connection: ' "No! No one has access to the secret of the future. Scarcely possible for even the most clairvoyant are certain presentiments, rapid glimpses, a vague and fugitive *coup d'œil*. The Revolution alone, as it clears the terrain, will reveal the horizon, will gradually remove the veils and open up the roads, or rather the multiple paths, that lead to the new order. Those who pretend to have in their pocket a complete map of this unknown land – they truly are madmen." Auguste Blanqui, *Critique sociale* (Paris, 1885), vol. 2, pp. 115–16 ("Les Sectes et la Révolution", October 1866).' W. Benjamin, *The Arcades Project*, p. 736.

6. I borrow here a formulation of Daniel Bensaïd's in his *Marx, l'intempestif*, p. 305.

7. 'Man defines himself by his project. This material being perpetually goes beyond the condition which is made for him; he reveals and determines his situation by transcending it in order to objectify himself – by work, action or gesture . . . As this impulse toward objectification assumes various forms according to the indivi-

dual, as it projects to us across a field of possibilities, some of which we realize to the exclusion of others, we call it also choice or freedom . . . What we call freedom is the irreducibility of the cultural order to the natural order.' Jean-Paul Sartre, *Search for a Method* (1960), trans. Hazel E. Barnes (New York: Vintage Books, 1963), pp. 150–2. Sartre never knew the writings of Walter Benjamin, but it would be interesting to compare their – admittedly, very different – conceptions of 'open history'. It goes without saying that the existentialism of the former was very far removed from the latter's Jewish messianism.

8. As Hannah Arendt writes, in an essay with the Benjaminian title 'The Concept of History': 'Unpredictability is not lack of foresight and no engineering management of human affairs will ever be able to eliminate it . . . Only total conditioning, that is, the total abolition of action, can ever hope to cope with unpredictability.' Hannah Arendt, 'The Concept of History: Ancient and Modern', *Between Past and Future* (New York: Penguin Books, 1993), p. 60.

9. 'It is beyond doubt that the capacity to act is the most dangerous of all human abilities and possibilities, and it is also beyond doubt that the self-created risks mankind faces today have never been faced before' (Hannah Arendt, 'The Concept of History', p. 63). It is clear that Arendt was influenced by Benjamin's 'Theses' – which she quotes at times – even if her general philosophical approach and political conclusions in no way coincide with those of her friend from Parisian exile.

10. See my essay 'Goldmann et Lukács: la vision du monde tragique', in F. Ferrarotti et al., *Le Structuralisme génétique: Goldmann* (Paris: Denoël/Gonthier, 1977).

11. As Miguel Abensour rightly observes, it is not utopia that is generative of totalitarianism, but a society without utopianism that is in danger of becoming a totalitarian society, caught up, as it is, in the dangerous illusion of completion. See M. Abensour, *L'Utopie, de Thomas More à Walter Benjamin* (Paris: Sens & Tonka, 2000), p. 19. Abensour argues that the hatred of utopia is a 'repetitive symptom which, from generation to generation, affects the defenders of the existing order, who are prey to the fear of otherness'.

12. A. Heller, 'Der Bahnhof als Metapher. Eine Betrachtung über die beschleunigte Zeit und die Endstationen der Utopie', *Frankfurter Rundschau*, 26 October 1991.

13. In an age like our own, whose Burkean logic makes progress/maturation an alibi for an unimaginative conservatism, Benjamin's theses reactivate this heterodox tradition already expressed by Mary Wollstonecraft in her *A Vindication of the Rights of Men*, for whom progress is an interruption of historical continuity, a *possibility* which emerges – not from the evolution of customs and institutions, but from the capacity of the human being to *tear itself away from the authority of custom* and open itself up to a new beginning. Far from functioning as 'fingerposts . . . to point out the right road', 'inherited experience would rather serve as lighthouses, to warn us against dangerous

rocks or sandbanks'. Mary Wollstonecraft, *A Vindication of the Rights of Men. A Letter to the Right Honourable Edmund Burke*, ed. J. Todd and M. Butler (London: W. Pickering, 1989), p. 41. See also Françoise Colin, Eveline Pisier and Eleni Varikas, *Les Femmes, de Platon à Derrida* (Paris: Plon, 2000), p. 410.

14. W. Benjamin, 'Paralipomena', *SW*, 4, p. 402.

15. Like Benjamin, Lucien Goldmann did not hesitate to reformulate historical materialism with the aid of concepts that were theological in origin. 'Marxist faith is faith in the *historical future* which men make themselves. Or, more accurately, in the future that *we* must make for ourselves by what we do, a "wager" on the success of our actions. The transcendental element present in this faith is not supernatural and does not take us outside or beyond history; it merely takes us beyond the individual.' L. Goldmann, *The Hidden God* (London: Routledge & Kegan Paul, 1964), p. 90 (translation modified). See my article, 'Le pari communautaire de Lucien Goldmann', *Recherche sociale*, 135, 1995.

16. K. Marx, 'Critique of Hegel's *Philosophy of Right*. Introduction', *Early Writings*, p. 251. ('Alle Verhältnisse umwerfen, in denen der Mensch ein erniedrigtes, ein geknechtetes, ein verlassenes, ein verächtliches Wesen ist.' *Zur Kritik der Hegelschen Rechtsphilosophie, Einleitung*, in MEGA, I, p. 385.)

17. 'Marxists do not combat exploitation, oppression, massive violence against human beings and injustice on a grand scale because that struggle fosters the development of the productive forces or of a narrowly defined historical progress . . . Even less do they combat these phenomena solely insofar as it has been scientifically demonstrated that the struggle will end with the victory of socialism. They combat exploitation, oppression, injustice and alienation as inhuman, shameful conditions. These are sufficient foundation and reason to do so.' Ernest Mandel, 'Die zukünftige Funktion des Marxismus', in H. Spatzenegger (ed.), *Das verspielte 'Kapital'? Die marxistische Ideologie nach dem Scheitern des Realen Sozialismus* (Salzburg: Verlag Anton Pustet, 1991), p. 173.

18. I borrow here a proposition advanced by Daniel Singer in his recent book *Whose Millennium? Theirs or Ours?* (New York: Monthly Review Press, 2000), pp. 272–3.

19. As Eleni Varikas points out, 'The fact that we are situated in the uncertainty of the present, that is to say, in a position from where we cannot foresee the consequences our actions and decisions will have for the future, allows us to conceive each historical moment as a present that opens out on to several futures. That is to say, to approach the past as a field of possibilities by attempting to localize the factors which enabled certain of those possibilities to be fulfilled to the exclusion of all the others.' E. Varikas, *Me diaforetiko prosopo. Filo, Diafora ke Oekumenikotita* (Athens: Katarti, 2000), p. 32.

20. *The Arcades Project*, pp. 809–11.

21. 'Their crafts and traditions may have been dying. Their hostility to the new industrialism may have been backward-looking. Their communitarian ideals may have been fantasies. Their insurrectionary conspiracies may have been foolhardy. But . . . in some of the lost causes of the people of the Industrial Revolution we may discover insights into social evils which we have yet to cure.' E. P. Thompson, *The Making of the English Working Class* (Harmondsworth: Penguin, 1968), p. 13.

Index

Printed in the United States
by Baker & Taylor Publisher Services

Revolutionary critic of the philosophy of progress, nostalgic of the past yet dreaming of the future, romantic partisan of materialism — Walter Benjamin is in every sense of the word an "unclassifiable" philosopher. His essay "On the Concept of History" was written in a state of urgency, as he attempted to escape the Gestapo in 1940, before finally committing suicide.

In this scrupulous, clear and fascinating examination of this essay, Michael Löwy argues that it remains one of the most important philosophical and political writings of the twentieth century. Looking in detail at Benjamin's celebrated but often mysterious text, and restoring the philosophical, theological and political context, Löwy highlights the complex relationship between redemption and revolution in Benjamin's philosophy of history.

"*Löwy's close reading … follows Benjamin's text thesis–by–thesis, bringing out the salient criticisms of orthodox Marxist discourse and highlighting the interruptions of this discourse, the interruption of the concept of time that is at its foundation, through Benjamin's insertion of messianic time into the banality of progress.*"
— *Jewish Quarterly*

"*Sensitive to Benjamin's profound anxiety and the tragic vision of the world, Löwy traces the unfurling of this 'revolutionary melancholia,' which is haunted by the recurrence of disasters … It is unusual to explore the depths of a text in this manner, but it is true that we have here the text of an exceptional thinker.*"
— *Le Monde*

ISBN 978-1-78478-641-0

51995

Philosophy
$19.95/$25.95CAN
versobooks.com

Cover Design & Art: Corporation Pop

9 781784 786410